Is There
Life After Divorce
in the Church?

Richard Lyon Morgan

Foreword by William V. Arnold

John Knox Press
ATLANTA

Library of Congress Cataloging in Publication Data

Morgan, Richard Lyon, 1929–
  Is there life after divorce in the church?

  Bibliography: p.
  Includes indexes.
  1. Divorce—Religious aspects—Christianity.
2. Clergy—Divorce. I. Title.

BT707.M67 1985   234'.165   85-42825
ISBN 0-8042-1123-X

© copyright John Knox Press 1985
10 9 8 7 6 5 4 3 2 1
Printed in the United States of America
John Knox Press
Atlanta, Georgia 30365

Acknowledgments

Unless otherwise indicated, Scripture quotations are from the Revised Standard Version of the Holy Bible, copyright, 1946, 1952, and © 1971, 1973 by the Division of Christian Education, National Council of the Churches of Christ in the U.S.A., and used by permission.

Some of the material in this book first appeared in the article "A Ritual of Remarriage" in the December 1983 issue of the *Journal of Pastoral Care*. Copyright © 1983 by the Association for Clinical Pastoral Education, Inc. and reprinted by permission.

Acknowledgment is made for excerpt from "How Heavy the Days" from POEMS by Hermann Hesse, selected and translated by James Wright. Copyright © 1970 by James Wright. Reprinted by permission of Farrar, Straus and Giroux, Inc.

Acknowledgment is made for excerpt from STAGES, from THE GLASS BEAD GAME by Hermann Hesse, translated by Richard and Clara Winston. Copyright © 1969 by Richard and Clara Winston. Reprinted by permission of Holt, Rinehart, and Winston, Inc.

Acknowledgment is made for "A Service of Divorce" by Henry T. Close in *Pilgrimage* 5 (Spring 1977), Human Sciences Press, Inc., New York. Copyright © Henry T. Close. Reprinted by permission of Human Sciences Press.

Acknowledgment is made for "Prayer for the Divorced" from *Rebel, O Jews!* by Mitchell Salem Fisher. Copyright © 1973 by Mitchell Salem Fisher. Reprinted by permission of Reconstructionist Press, Inc.

Acknowledgment is made for the MSI Scale of the MARITAL STATUS INVENTORY. Reprinted with permission from Weiss, R. L. & Cerreto, M. C. "The Marital Status Inventory: Development of a Measure of Dissolution Potential." *The American Journal of Family Therapy*, 1980, 8(2), 80–85, © Brunner/Mazel, Inc.

Acknowledgment for use of excerpts from other copyrighted materials:

Abingdon Press, from THE DIVORCING CHRISTIAN by Lewis R. Rambo. Copyright © 1983. Reprinted by permission of Abingdon Press.

Basic Books, Inc., from MARITAL SEPARATION by Robert S. Weiss. Copyright © 1975 by Basic Books, Inc.

The Christian Century Foundation, from "A THEOLOGY OF DIVORCE" by Robert F. Sinks. Copyright 1984 Christian Century Foundation. Reprinted by permission from the April 20, 1977 issue of The Christian Century.

Doubleday, Inc., excerpt from THE WOUNDED HEALER by Henri Nouwen. Copyright © 1972 by Henri J. M. Nouwen. Reprinted by permission of Doubleday & Company, Inc.

Alfred A. Knopf, Inc., from THE PLAGUE by Albert Camus. Translated by Stuart Gilbert. Copyright © 1969. Reprinted by permission of Alfred A. Knopf, Inc.

University of Notre Dame, from "A Christian Understanding of Divorce" by Thomas M. Olshewsky in the *Journal of Religious Ethics* 7 (Spring 1979). Copyright © 1979 Religious Ethics, Inc.

William Morrow & Company, Inc., from A SECOND DAY by Robert Farrar Capon. Copyright © 1980. Reprinted by permission of William Morrow & Company, Inc.

Winston Press, from LITURGY & LEARNING THROUGH THE LIFE CYCLE by John H. Westerhoff III and William H. Willimon. Copyright Winston/Seabury. Published by Winston Press, 430 Oak Grove, Minneapolis, MN 55403 (formerly published by The Seabury Press). All rights reserved. Used with permission.

Introduction

You may be reading this book because you feel powerless to help friends or family who go through divorce. I know how you feel. There have been times when I was so embarrassed for people experiencing separation that I avoided them. You may be reading this book because your marriage is in trouble and divorce is a possible option. I know how you feel. I, too, struggled with this agonizing decision which can be made only by the individual. You may be a minister, to whom many divorcing people turn for a word beyond despair. I know how you feel. I have stood speechless in homes when families were breaking up, and children were feeling like pieces of paper torn in two. You may be already divorced. I also know how *you* feel. This book records some of my own divorce journey, an amazing story of death and resurrection. Whoever you are, if divorce has ever touched your life, this is a book for you.

This book does not condone divorce for Christians, but seeks to deal with the issues divorced Christians face once divorce has happened to them. It does not deal with the serious questions about children of divorce. Those questions are monumental and could not be handled within the scope of this book. However, it is my belief that when parents work through the problems of a divorce, their children's adjustment is made easier. As Joseph Epstein says, "In divorce there are only smaller and larger disasters." If adults work through the large problems, divorce may be a "smaller disaster" for children.

This book offers hope to the divorced and to the church. For the divorced, so often the victims of polite silence or overt rejection in the church, it offers a theology that promises "a third day" to those who do the hard work of penitence, who grow through their divorce, not merely go through it. For the church member and minister, wanting to help divorced persons rather than to hurt them, this book offers some constructive suggestions for ministry. I believe most church people do care, but lack the knowledge and skills for ministry to the divorced.

My thanks go to a number of persons who made this publication possible: to my wife Alice Ann, who helped me work through my divorce and this manuscript with grace and hope; to Anne Ferraro, who typed the manuscript numerous times; to John Gibbs of John Knox Press, who made many helpful suggestions and has been a constant support; to Joan Crawford and Ginger Pyron of John Knox Press, who shared the task of producing the final version of the manuscript and made "the rough places plain;" to the members of Fairview Presbyterian Church, Lenoir, North Carolina, whose patience with their pastor made this book possible; and finally, to all the divorced Christians who made me feel their need and the church's responsibility.

This book calls to the divorced Christian that it is time to "return home" to the church. Isaiah's words knock gently at our hearts:

Comfort, comfort my people,
    says your God.
Speak tenderly to Jerusalem,
    and cry to her
that her warfare is ended,
    that her iniquity is pardoned,
that she has received from the LORD's hand
    double for all her sins.
                    (Isa. 40:1–2)

There are no rigid guidelines for learning from divorce; each individual perceives it from the vantage point of his or her values and history. However, in sharing their experiences and in realizing the compassion of Christ, individuals may come to learn from each other. If *Is There Life After Divorce in the Church?* underscores what is common to every divorce journey and speaks a word of grace and hope, it will have served its author well.

Foreword

With its great increase in frequency and visibility over recent decades, divorce has held a central place for discussion and debate in the church. The numbers of books on the topic give further evidence of the interest, accompanied by discomfort, among scholars, pastors, and congregations. In many ways, the question is still just as strong—"What do we do with divorce in the church?" More importantly, "How do we deal with those in the church who are divorced?"

Church publications on the issue tend to be fairly narrow in their scope. Some will move through careful exegetical study of Scripture for a "position." Others will advance a cause in almost polemic terms. Still others become how-to manuals, treating the issue as one more task to be turned into a program. All are useful in their own way, but seldom do writers take up the integration of the various pieces of the issue.

Richard Morgan is attempting to take on that integrative task in this book, and for his willingness to do so, I am grateful. He brings to his writing an important blend of credentials. An ordained minister, he has been trained in more rigorous contexts than most through carrying out not only the work of a basic degree but that of an academic doctorate as well. There is no way for him to avoid coming to terms with biblical and theological issues in the struggle with divorce. Beyond the personal experience of theological education is a family tradition of which ministry is a part; it is "in his genes," so to speak. Further, he has received training in pastoral care and counseling. His academic experience has been balanced by the clinical pilgrimage of finding ways to live out all those ideas in the gutsy areas of human existence.

All those credentials of family and education are adequate to qualify someone for a writing task, but Dick brings another ingredient. He is divorced and remarried. His work is not that of the interested and sensitive scholar/pastor alone—it is also that of the healing victim. A blend of voices can be heard in his work.

Readers of this book will find points of very real discomfort. They will not get the mild, gentle, assuring encouragement to "be sensitive." Many of the words convey a sense of the anger behind the thin veneer of those who are divorced. There are accusations. We, the church, which includes the divorced, have been trapped by what we perceive as a conflict between commitment to marriage and commitment to caring for those who divorce. Thus, we often are seduced into choosing one or the other. On the one hand, in a quick attempt to comfort, we may imply that anything goes. On the other hand, in an attempt to affirm our belief in the sanctity of marriage, we may imply that forgiveness is not to be found for those who choose, for whatever reasons, to divorce and perhaps remarry.

There is no lasting comfort in an approach that says "anything is OK—just don't tell me too much about it!" Neither is there any sensitivity in a response that has only one criterion for acceptance: stay married. As a matter of fact, both approaches depend on "staying out of it" as a means of staying pure. The struggle with purity is not a new issue in the church, but it hurts all the more when we find that we have slipped into it unawares.

The power of this book is its attempt to struggle with all those issues and more. Dick Morgan does not allow us to escape facing the inconsistencies of our behavior in the church, nor does he allow us to miss the experience of those who have felt excluded. That is where the anger comes through. At the same time, the divorced and those who plan to remarry are not let off the hook. They are called to accountability as well.

Most important to me, Dick attempts to deal realistically with the theological implications that lie deep within the issues of divorce and remarriage. This book is not a call to arms that comes *only* out of strong emotion and sensitive understanding of the pain involved. It is a call that rightly expects us to look more closely at the theological underpinnings for what we do. The question of the church's response to the divorced and the remarried is not simply a "social" question, nor is it merely a question of "rights." Although those questions are important, we are dealing fundamentally with a theological issue. Whether we are divorced or single or married, our response to divorce and remarriage is one evidence of our belief about the nature of our living together as a human community that seeks to be faithful to a very particular kind of God. Every form of reaching out or pulling in, every ritual in which we engage, from baptism to marriage to divorce to remarriage, is a commentary on what we believe. This book is a call to faithfulness, and that is never crystal clear. It calls us to wrestle together.

As you move through these pages, plan to be a little upset. Plan to get a little angry or frustrated. Plan to take another look at your faith and at some very specific things you can do as expressions of your commitment to caring within the church, whether you are single, married, divorced, or remarried.

—William V. Arnold
Professor of Pastoral Care and Counseling
Union Theological Seminary in Virginia

Contents

To
those who still sit
in the darkness of divorce
and
Alice Ann
who helped me realize
"A Third Day"

I.

A Nagging Issue: Divorced Persons in the Church

Archaic Ideas About Divorce

One of the lingering problems that faces the Christian church is what to do with divorced persons. Like the nagging widow in Jesus' parable, who pestered the unjust judge until he vindicated her, divorced persons still haunt the church with their cries for justice and compassion. Formerly, the church adopted a "priest and Levite attitude" toward divorced people, and politely walked by on the other side of their pain. It was not too many years ago that divorce was discussed behind closed doors; it was shocking to meet a divorced person on the street, unthinkable in the church. The ministry of the church was restricted to intact families, with token programs for the single unmarrieds and the widows. But all that has changed with the rising divorce rate and the millions of divorced persons who are in the church. The "polite silence" still prevails in some church circles; one divorcée told me, "I wish that some of the members would express their feelings about my separation. Anger or sadness would be a lot better than this awful silence and embarrassment."

When the church does respond to divorced persons, it often oscillates between two extremes, a "cheap grace acceptance" on the one hand and "a cold shoulder rejection" on the other. William V. Arnold has pointed out this polarization:

> If a church says there is no room for divorced persons because they are wrong, there is a painful absence of the New Testament emphasis on forgiveness. On the other hand, if there is a blissful, passive, unconcerned acceptance of divorced persons, there is an equally painful absence of caring enough to encourage growth.[1]

At times the church tries to be kind to divorcing persons, but at other times its negligence is downright inhuman. Vidal S. Clay describes the painful difference she noticed on the occasion of her separation as compared with her previous experience of bereavement after her first husband died.[2] Her son's words, "Where are the neighbors bringing in food?" reminded her of the support the family had received when her husband died—a support that was noticeably absent when they were left alone again because of separation.

Many in the church still cling to archaic ideas about divorce. Divorce is seen as an enemy, an anarchism of the worst kind. The classic sociological works on divorce, which are still influential in American life, incorporate this antidivorce bias.[3] Margaret Mead summed up this bias when she wrote,

> In measuring the breakdown of society, it is customary for researchers to group together statistics on crime, juvenile delinquency, addiction, mental illness, and divorce.[4]

Those divorcing are led to believe that breaking up is not only a painful and debilitating experience, but an insurmountable disaster, and that little community or church support is available. William B. Oglesby, Jr. has pointed out that some of those feelings of hurt and embarrassment are misperceptions: "Somehow these people seemed to feel or were made to feel that they were disqualified as human beings and as members of the church by reason of the failure in their marriages."[5] But the fact remains that they do feel betrayed, rejected, and unwanted. As Dory Krongelb Beatrice has said,

> In spite of the increasing acceptance of divorce in our society, many vestiges of stigma remain which label divorced persons as deviants, misfits, failures, or threats to intact marriages.[6]

Nowhere is this antidivorce bias more evident than in the church. Traditionalists still call for strict opposition to divorce on biblical grounds. The attitude in the earlier American religious community was simple and clear: since marriage is sacred, it must be defended and preserved. Divorce is an enemy to be avoided at any cost. Witness Edith Wharton's novel *Ethan Frome* (1911), in which the title character is locked into an intolerable marriage to his wife Zeena and cannot divorce to marry his lover, Mattie Silver. He considers divorce by fleeing to the West with Mattie, but cannot, owing to both poverty and his Puritan conscience. He cannot betray this religious tradition, even if it has made a ruin out of his life. Rigid responsibility, however demeaning and dehumanizing, must take precedence over personal freedom. Little wonder that the vestiges of this antidivorce bias have left divorced persons in the church feeling guilty, alienated, and shut out. They may have experienced some life after divorce, but a lurking feeling remains that some sacred code has been violated and God's will disobeyed.

Changes have taken place in many religious circles in the last twenty years, and it is time that the church recognize and affirm these changes. Forgiveness and restoration have come to take precedence over blaming and pronouncing judgment. The decision to divorce may in a given situation be an appropriate act of Christian faith and conscience, and the experience of working through the crisis of divorce, however painful and dislocating, an occasion of personal and spiritual growth. Central to this new approach in the church is the belief that divorce can be a redemptive process in which God's grace and truth are manifest. Robert F. Sinks, a Methodist minister, describes this change:

> When continuation in an unfulfilling or destructive marriage thwarts and crushes human lives, then provision must be made for ending that marriage. Sometimes divorce may be little other than an escape from the intolerable. On other occasions it may be a clear and creative movement toward fulfillment through which persons recognize that their present relationship no longer gives hope to the growing potentialities of either partner.[7]

Monsignor Stephen J. Kelleher of the Roman Catholic Church expressed his liberalized view of divorce when he wrote, "No bond is sacred which dehumanizes the persons bound. There is no sign of Christ in a marriage in which the parties are destroying each other."[8] A theology of divorce is desperately needed for divorced persons in the church who still have to combat the view that divorce is an unforgivable sin.

The Rising Divorce Rate

No matter how it is measured, the incidence of divorce in the United States has risen rapidly in the last twenty years. Statistics have been kept in America since 1867, and with the exception of a few interludes, the divorce rate has climbed steadily since then, rising more than 300% between 1890 and 1970. In 1975 there were over a million divorces in America (1,026,000), which is twice as many divorces as in 1966 and three times as many as in 1955. The divorce rate for 1983 was 5.1 divorces granted for every 1,000 Americans, a total of 1,180,000 divorces.

Although it is true that these figures reflect the first slight decline of the divorce rate in two decades, that decline can be misleading. In 1983 there were 1.2 million couples who ended their marriages, a highly significant number. One of the reasons cited for the slight decline in the divorce rate was that more young couples were living together before making a decision about marriage, and thus their rate of "divorce" was not reflected in divorce statistics. Also cited was the recession of 1982, which caused many deadlocked marriages to continue because the couples could not afford to get divorced. They postponed separation or divorce because of job uncertainty and the expense of maintaining another residence. But economists and social scientists predict that the divorce rate will rise again if the economy does well, and that by 1990 it may be at an all-time high.

The church must face the facts that there is still one divorce for every two marriages, an increase from one divorce per six marriages in 1930, and that more and more children are involved in marital disruption. It is estimated that 40% of the children born during the 1970s will be involved in divorce before reaching the age of 18. What is the church's responsibility for adults and children whose lives have been torn apart by divorce?

These divorce statistics do not mean that the family is "falling apart" or that the institution of marriage is "on the way out." There was a record 2.5 million marriages in 1982, up 2% from the previous year. And 32% of these marriages are remarriages. As Andrew J. Cherlin says,

> The upshot of all this is that most people who get divorced remarry. About five out of six men and about three out of four women remarry after a divorce. . . . And those who are going to remarry do so soon after their divorce: about half of all remarriages take place within three years after divorce.[9]

What the data suggest is that people now expect to receive more from marriage and are less willing to settle for relationships that do not measure up to expectations. The church and society at large need to help people encountering this powerful and shaking experience of change. There are still no religiously or socially sanctioned rituals to function as "rites of passage," and relatively few support systems for divorcing people. The legal process does not provide a socially approved outlet for the volatile emotions that are present during the early stages of separation. As sociologist Paul Bohannan puts it, "Divorces are 'cranked out' but divorcees are not 'cooled out.'"[10]

Myths and Misconceptions

Myths are unsubstantiated beliefs that are accepted uncritically by society. There are few social realities more prone to myths and misconceptions than divorce. Church members tend to accept such myths about divorce as: "Divorced persons are psychologically sick." "Divorced persons expect greater freedom and self-discovery without paying the price of growth." "Divorced persons always want to get remarried." "There are always a victim and a villain in divorce." "Only women experience emotional problems in divorce." "Nice Christians do not get divorced." "Divorce does not happen to clergy." It is time to look beyond these myths and deal with divorce on a more realistic basis.

(1) Divorced persons are psychologically sick. Psychiatrist Edmund Bergler argues that all people who divorce have character disorders or neuroses. He claims that unconscious motivation informs choice of the marriage partner, and it is fallacious to think that one solves problems by leaving the marriage and finding another spouse. The chances are high, he writes, that one will select another tormentor for the same reasons. Bergler maintained that "where a neurosis is involved, divorce will not correct the cause of marriage failure. . . . The partner is changed—that's the only difference."[11]

No one will deny that divorcing people experience a "crazy time." In fact, Abigail Trafford's book *Crazy Time* makes it clear that anyone who is "normal" in this time of stress is really crazy. People tend to regress to lower levels of functioning during a divorce. This "craziness" starts at the initial separation and usually lasts about two years. "It's a time when your emotions take on a life of their own and you swing back and forth between wild euphoria and violent anger, ambivalence and deep depression, extreme timidity and rash actions. You are not yourself."[12] But in no sense is this "craziness" to be equated with a full-blown psychological illness.

Many people do divorce and remarry in an attempt to solve old conflicts. Unconsciously, some people do select new partners who will bring into their lives therapy for some of the problems which earlier had led to divorce. But in reality, it takes strength and courage to work through a divorce and forge a new life. Divorce is a small death, because the experience involves dying to the past, learning new skills, and seeking self-renewal.

The seeds of growth and re-establishment are present in every separation, but only strong persons can successfully cultivate them. Rather than viewing divorce as an irresponsible act, I believe that it is often only the strong who choose to separate and work through the pain, instead of remaining psychological cripples in an oppressive marriage. In many cases, the in-between time becomes the space needed for overcoming past conflicts and entertaining a second marriage with no illusions and a far more realistic understanding of the marriage bond. One minister commented,

> I've had a much higher degree of success in marrying couples, one or both of whom have been married before, than marrying couples both of whom are being married for the first time. The former seem more often to have their feet on the ground and to have counted the cost of marriage better.

(2) *Divorced persons expect greater freedom and self-discovery without paying the price of growth.* Many couples who divorce expect less stress and conflict, along with more joy and fulfillment. With such a "happily-ever-after" attitude, few are prepared for the traumas and stress they experience. The problem is aggravated by the delayed reaction to stress which often ensues. The initial feelings of relief soon fade, and serious emotional and physical problems can occur. Esther Oshiver Fisher calls divorce "the death of a marriage," in which "the husband and wife together with their children are the mourners . . . the court is the cemetery where the coffin is sealed and the dead marriage buried."[13] On the Social Readjustment Rating Scale of Thomas H. Holmes and Richard H. Rahe, divorce is second only to death of a spouse in the amount of stress it produces. When resultant factors are considered (separation, change in financial state, change in living conditions, etc.), it ranks the most stressful of all human conditions.[14] The fact that divorce is now discussed openly makes it no less traumatic. Divorce can be a positive solution to a conflict-ridden marriage, but it is a fallacy to idealize the divorce process without taking into account its attendant grief. E. Mavis Hetherington, Martha Cox, and Roger Cox studied families of divorce and concluded,

We didn't find a single victimless divorce among the families we studied. At least one member of each family reported distress or showed a negative change in behavior. . . . Most of them were ultimately able to cope with their problems, but the adjustment was often unexpectedly painful.[15]

The attitude that single-again people are "swingers" often prevails among church folk. Married people in the church often have problems inviting divorced friends to dinner without finding someone of the opposite sex to balance out the number of couples. Separated church members are often suspect at church gatherings, since some assume they are looking for matches, and hence, are disruptive. One divorced woman put it this way:

I find myself in a catch-22 situation with my church friends. On the one hand, my single-again state threatens my friends who think I want to snatch their husbands, and on the other hand, they have to match me up to make me normal. Why can't they just let me be single?

(3) Divorced persons always want to get remarried. The prevalent American myth of success means that being happily married is an integral part of the good life. This myth sweeps into the church and makes divorced persons feel abnormal unless they are searching for a new partner. Church people often get into the matchmaking business, not realizing that this behavior may be offensive and dehumanizing to their separated friends. Divorced clergy have to face the reality that remarried clergy are perceived with less suspicion than are those that have not remarried, and that they apparently have more upward career mobility. One minister, who declined to become involved in the Presbyterian Association for Divorced Clergy, explained:

I can remember how hard it was for me to stay in the parish when I was divorced, or to get a call elsewhere. It's not that I don't want to help your cause, but for my own protection, I must keep silent. My church doesn't even know I am divorced and remarried.

This "mix and match" ideology is a disservice to newly single persons. Singleness is not a disease for which remarriage is the cure. The church is not ministering to divorced persons if its only concern is to get them remarried. It is sad that if churches do recognize the needs of divorced members at all, they tend to organize events for them in order that the newly single can meet and marry, and therefore fit comfortably into the life of the church.

(4) *There are always a victim and a villain in divorce.* Usually the spouse who leaves the marriage becomes the villain, and the one who is left is viewed as the helpless victim whose life has been shattered by the errant spouse. Those who leave the marriage may be overcome with unnecessary guilt. As one woman put it, "I had to make this hard decision to leave our marriage, but I still feel guilty about it, even though it has been the best decision I ever made." Dumpers often carry a burden of considerable guilt, while dumpees usually feel rejected. Bruce Fisher distinguishes between *good-dumpers and bad-dumpers*, and between *good-dumpees and bad-dumpees*.[16] Good-dumpers work hard on the marriage to make it last, but finally realize that the relationship was destructive to both persons and that separation is a healthy decision. Bad-dumpers are similar to runaway kids; they avoid the problems of marriage and always choose flight in response to difficulties. Good-dumpees are not mere "innocent victims," since they too have contributed to the problems of the relationship; however, they are basically mismatched with the dumpers, and even if they are willing to go for marriage counseling, they may simply be at the wrong time and place. Bad-dumpees are people who want to be out of marriage but do not have the courage and strength to be dumpers. Most people who separate—both dumpers and dumpees—are a combination of Fisher's good and bad types.

The truth is that there is no culprit when divorce occurs. The many contributing factors can never be known, so it is a waste of energy to blame someone or talk about who is the "innocent" partner. Both spouses need to take the responsibility for the dissolution of a marriage. The myth of victim and villain is accentuated in the church when a minister and spouse divorce. Members of the congregation choose up sides in the conflict, and it is little wonder that some divorcing clergy feel they must resign.

(5) Only women experience emotional problems in divorce. One would think from listening to many divorced men that only women suffer when divorce occurs. No one denies the shattering impact of divorce on women. Mel Krantzler, who describes his own traumatic divorce, emphasizes that

> Few men have to cope with the problems of the divorced mother trying to juggle her maternal responsibilities with her need to work and establish a new social life. The divorced man may never experience the same degree of fear and uncertainty as the middle-aged divorced woman with grown-up children who is suddenly thrown back into a world which places such a high premium on youth and good looks.[17]

However, men suffer from divorce too, despite the machismo myth that men do not hurt. They have reactions similar to those of women, experiencing failure, rejection, and hurt. The stages of divorce (discussed in Chapter II) are as real for men as they are for women. The great number of clergymen who have been open about the painful process of divorce has served to explode this myth. Hetherington, Cox, and Cox compared seventy-two middle-class, married couples with the same number of divorced couples in which the mother had custody of the children. These researchers concluded,

> The divorced fathers' increased distress, disorganized lifestyle, and frantic social activity immediately after divorce seems to be a way of trying new methods of exploring and coping with the unexpected problems of divorce. . . . their continuing problems show that many have not yet completely escaped the aftermath of divorce.[18]

Men face deep loss and dependency when they are plunged suddenly into an entirely new lifestyle. Consider the plight of a divorced clergyman, whose wife left him the single parent of three adolescents. He expressed his feelings this way:

> People in the church have been very helpful and understanding. But the stress of ministering to a large congregation and suddenly being the sole parent of three teenagers is an overload of stress.

I'm handling it now, but what will it be like when the delayed reaction to all this takes place?

As the long-dominant macho image begins to decline and more men feel secure in being open about their feelings instead of hiding behind an armor of traditional masculinity, the word will get out that when marriages are disrupted, men hurt, too.

(6) *Nice Christians do not get divorced.* One of the prevailing myths in the church about divorce is that "nice Christians do not get divorced." Divorce is only for those "bad" people outside the church, and unthinkable for a Christian. "If good Christians do not get a divorce, and I got a divorce, then I must not be a good Christian" is the way some people put it together. They reason that all the pain, rejection, and condemnation they feel are punishment for sins. As Lewis R. Rambo puts it,

> Some churches tend to be very harsh both on the issue of divorce and on church members who resort to it. Sometimes we have nowhere to turn because most of our friends are Christians who reject our action, so our sense of isolation grows. In addition, some of our churches and friends tell us, "good Christians" do not have emotional problems . . . and "good Christians" certainly never get a divorce.[19]

It is a strange anomaly that the church can forgive all kinds of offenses and yet consider divorce an outrage.

(7) *Divorce does not happen very often to clergy.* Divorce among the clergy remains the "closet problem" of the church, since many church members are offended and shocked by it. Divorce *may* be acceptable for some people, they acknowledge, but certainly never for the clergyperson whose marriage must be a model of connubial bliss. Laity expect their ministers to have successful, productive, and happy marriages. They would be horrified to discover sobering statistics on the increasing incidence of clergy divorce. Paul Glick, retired senior demographer at the Bureau of Census, told me that in 1960 the divorce rate for clergy was 0.2%. By 1970 it had doubled to 0.4%. Some authorities predict that the number of divorced clergy may one day equal the percentage found in the general population. Lyle E. Schaller, church consultant with the Yokefellow Institute, re-

cently stated, "My hunch is that one-fourth of the ordained clergy either have been divorced or will see their marriages end in divorce rather than death."[20] Clergy divorce *is* a growing reality.

Ministry to the New Gentiles

What I am saying is that in spite of prejudice within the church, divorce now has become a likelihood for many Christians. Church members will no longer remain in sterile marriages for the children's sake or for "religious" reasons. Many Christians even view their courage to divorce as an act of responsible Christian commitment. The divorce rate dropped slightly in 1982 because of the economic recession, but that may be only a temporary decline. Social pressures for remaining within a deadlocked marriage are lessening, old religious taboos are disappearing, and penalties for departure have diminished. Divorce now touches almost everyone in the church. A thirty-five-year-old college professor explains how the married adults of his Young Adult Class felt angry and threatened even when divorce was introduced as a topic for discussion:

> The reason some of us got so disturbed at the discussion of divorce is that unlike our classes on death, we could not dismiss it from our own situation. Death still seems so far away; divorce could happen to any of us.

Divorced people in the church still find themselves in a catch-22 situation. There does seem to be a greater tolerance for divorce, if only because of the "domino effect" (i.e., the more divorces among one's friends, the easier it is to envision divorce for oneself). However, traces of the old taboos and stigmas still remain. Divorced persons still feel like misfits in the church, belonging neither to the couples class nor to the never-married group of adults. They are tired of being channeled into such classes as Pairs and Spares, WARM (Women and Reluctant Males), and SCOUP (Single, Career and Obviously Unattached Persons).

A strange paradox has developed. The church claims it is the body of Christ, who in his earthly ministry was a magnet for people whose lives were broken and desperate. He also had some strong words to say to "religious people" who criticized him for associating with such folk. A striking reversal has taken place. Jesus offended the self-righteous and comforted the sinners, but today the church often coddles and caters to its "respectable" members, and from the sinners turns its face away. Nowhere is this more evident than in the attitude of the church toward the divorced. Although the church may not blatantly reject divorced persons, its token acceptance may put them on the defensive to prove they were the innocent party, or make its hidden agenda imply that no divorced person can hold office in the church.

If the church were in reality the "house of prayer for all people," then divorced persons would be welcome. Divorced persons can be termed "the new Gentiles" of the church. Like the ancient Gentiles, who at first were excluded from the church, many divorced persons do feel ignored, even unwanted, by church congregations. Like the Gentiles, who confronted the pristine Christian community with a challenge for ministry and were accepted only if they first became Jews (Gal. 2:11–22), divorced persons may feel that their acceptance in the church depends upon their getting remarried. In both ancient Galatia and modern America, this policy—whether expressly stated or merely implied—denies the gospel of grace.

It is obvious that the modern church has been as impervious to the pain of its divorced persons as was the early Christian church to the presence of the Gentiles. Like the Syrophoenician woman, however, divorced persons beg for crumbs from the table of the church, and the church must follow its Lord in surrendering to this persistent faith. The accidental integrated fellowship at Antioch, the timely conversion of Paul, and Peter's experience at Caesarea were all *kairos* moments which forced the church to deal with the inequity. The Christian church is still locked into ministry to its traditional membership, i.e., married people in families. Divorced persons feel like "fifth wheels" and "sore thumbs" in a Noah's Ark society. One divorcée put this exclusion quite well:

> I still feel like an outsider in my own church, and yet I go. The old medieval manuscript said it for me: "If it weren't for the storm outside, I couldn't stand the smell inside."

The analogy is a two-edged sword. The church *is* Noah's Ark in its insistence on retaining the vestiges of a couples-dominated culture and its preference for pairs. On the other hand, it is *unlike* Noah's Ark in being the Ark of Salvation, where divorced persons can experience wholeness (shalom) in the family of God. Divorced persons battle storms of loneliness and despair, which at times seem as overwhelming as flood waters, and yearn for the comfort and security of the church. Howard J. Clinebell, Jr., succinctly identifies the problem:

> A strong family-oriented emphasis unwittingly creates an excluding climate which tends to increase the heavy loneliness load of such persons. Meeting the needs of non-family persons is a challenge to any church. . . . this is the acid test of a church's person-centeredness. Can its group program be so varied, inclusive, and need-satisfying that it will provide a substitute family for the family-less?[21]

These words stand in judgment on the contemporary church, which claims to be "a house of prayer for all people." The few, sporadic attempts to minister to divorced persons have produced what Hendrika Vande Kemp and G. Peter Schreck call baptized "singles bars,"[22] i.e., isolated classes or groups which have no dynamic relation to the real life of the congregation.

Mainline Protestant churches still lag well behind in ministering to the "new Gentiles." The movie *Starting Over* provides a sad commentary on the church's failure in this regard. At the end of the film, two groups of divorced people meet in the basement of the church, segregated by sex and separated from other church members. As they sit and stare at each other in self-conscious pain and loneliness, the joyful music of Christmas is dimly heard above. A fellowship does emerge, as the two groups mingle and exchange their gifts of food and friendship, reminiscent of the gifts of the Magi; but the mainstream of church life and liturgy remains above, removed and aloof from the divorced persons' plight and pain.

Those who minister to divorced persons need to be aware of different stages in the divorce process. It is my belief that there is a great deal of difference between the earlier stages of divorce, the "crazy time," and the latter stages when the pain has abated. The earlier stage is a time of excruciating pain for Christians who divorce. Not only must each divorced person deal with his or her own problems, but each one also carries the extra burden of the Christian faith, which often condemns instead of consoles. Later on, however, there comes a time when the possibilities of a new life loom greater than the painful memories, and new directions open.

I will suggest creative ways in which the church can minister first to the early pain of the divorce process, all the confusion and craziness of those first weeks and months when life seems shattered beyond repair. "Is there any balm in Gilead?" divorced persons wonder. In the later chapters, I will focus on the reconstructing of life beyond divorce, when the newly single ask the question of Nicodemus: "How can a man be born when he is old?"

My Divorce Journey

This book is written from personal experience, both from my own divorce journey and from the stories of other divorced people with whom I have worked in the church. What Carl Rogers says is true: "That which is most personal is most universal." My experience will not parallel yours exactly, for everyone walks a separate road on this journey. I have simply tried to speak as a Christian who has struggled with divorce, and whose struggle may kindle a spark of identification with your own story. For those of you who have never been divorced, my story may help you understand the problems divorced persons face and may cause you to respond more compassionately to others who walk this road.

I was named Richard Lyon after an eminent American clergyman. At the hour of my birth in Lexington, Kentucky, my grandfather, Dr. G. Campbell Morgan, internationally known British expositor, was preaching a sermon at my father's church on the subject, "The New Birth." My parents constantly reminded me, that this coincidence had clearly marked me for the ministry. I was taught a literal interpretation of Scripture and introjected much of the fundamentalism of my parents. I rarely heard divorce discussed, and when it was mentioned, I felt it had to be an unforgivable sin which would damn offenders to everlasting hell. I remember that once my father refused to marry a couple in our church because both of them were divorced. I suspect that if I had met any divorced persons I would have "crossed by on the other side" for fear their evil would contaminate me.

I married too young, without understanding myself. I wanted the rewards of intimacy without the effort of self-knowledge. During my first pastorate in West Virginia, my marital problems began to surface. My low self-esteem and struggle with my past made me a difficult person. After leaving the ministry in 1959, telling my friends that "I wasn't defrocked; only unsuited," I threw myself into my career, and was not a good husband or father. I produced a best-selling textbook in psychology which paid the price of my divorce. Although my spouse and I tried counseling, erosion gave way to detachment, and in 1975 we separated, divorcing in 1976. I still recall the painful struggle of deciding whether to leave or not. I walked endless streets, finding no answers. I talked to divorced friends, seeking to justify my intentions, and planned my exit a million times. Eventually I did leave, but thoughts of my children pulled me back; I preferred a comfortable prison to the loneliness of freedom. It took a lot of work to overcome the feelings that divorce was an unforgivable sin, a scandal that would stigmatize my family and jeopardize my future. Finally, I made the move.

Single life was "crazy time," a strange yo-yo life between relief and despair. I spent months in an upstairs apartment, like Anne Frank filling endless journals with my thoughts. Two people became my spiritual guides: my brother John, who had walked a similar road and whose letters became messages of hope; and a blind friend named Jesse, who shared my burden and seemed to understand. I felt like one of the early Christians, trapped in a gray limbo between a past that had ended and a future that was yet unknown. I saw an old man shuffling down the street and felt that he was the mirror of my future—a man alone, rejected, and outcast. I tried to relate to a church, but felt "unwanted and unclean," and no one really seemed to have time for this outsider. It was the typical Noah's Ark society. In time I felt better, and began to reassess my goals.

I met Alice Ann, the widow of a Presbyterian minister, and our common pain became the birth of genuine intimacy. We were married by a Presbyterian minister who was highly supportive, and began the strange new life of a "reconstituted" family with no guidelines but our faith and love for each other.

In 1980 I returned to the parish ministry, finally "called" by God rather than by tradition. My experience had sensitized me to others' pain, and Henri J. M. Nouwen's "wounded healer" became my model of ministry. Much of my present ministry is to the broken, the dimly burning wicks and bruised reeds, the aged, the dying, the divorced, the distressed. My own fall from grace tempered me to be more compassionate to others who fail. I know what it means to be knocked down but not knocked out. My journey continues, but now I am surrounded by a constant awareness of the biblical truth, "If any one is in Christ, he is a new creation; the old has passed away, behold, the new has come" (2 Cor. 5:17).

The truth is all too apparent that in this country there are several million divorced people, many of whom sit in pews on Sunday morning or linger on church inactive rolls. Can the church pretend these people do not exist? Dare we imply that the church has a word only for the person who has never married, or whose marriage is intact? Are we to expunge the story of the woman at the well from our biblical canons? or the story of Hosea and Gomer? Is there a word from the Lord for divorced Christians, save overt tolerance or overt condemnation? Are divorced persons stuck forever with either a harsh intolerance or an unrealistic acceptance by church members? Will church members ever realize that divorce is neither to be treated lightly or condoned, nor is it to be regarded as unforgivable or condemned? Is there a more excellent way? These are the real questions of this book.

The church faces a dual problem. At times it has to address itself to marriages which are having difficulty standing the strain of expectations for personal fulfillment. Elaine Tyler May, commenting on the way that personal fulfillment seems to have become a national obsession in twentieth-century America, says,

> It is not likely that the domestic domain will ever be able to satisfy completely the great expectations for individual fulfillment brought to it. As long as the American pursuit of happiness continues along this private path, divorce is likely to be with us.[23]

The church has to make it clear that the breaking of a sacred union does in fact matter and that commitment is still a vital part of the marriage covenant.

On the other hand, the church must reckon with many divorced persons who feel like publicans in the parish. Like the ancient publican, who stood afar off in the temple, hurt and broken by his own sense of unworthiness and shame, divorced persons stand outside the mainstream of life in the church, waiting to hear that liberating Word, "This man went down to his house justified" (Luke 18:14). Pastoral theologian Wayne E. Oates has clarified this balanced ministry of the church to the divorced:

> . . . the church and its ministry are responsible for the rehabilitation of divorced and remarried couples in ways that neither compromise the integrity of the Christian ideal of marriage as a permanent covenant between two Christians nor consider the remarried persons as being sinners in a way that is either unpardonable or unique as contrasted with the other sinners in the fellowship of the forgiven.[24]

A new climate of hope and optimism is developing for people who divorce. Divorce can be seen as a healthy, courageous, liberating, even Christian act. Still, however, too much apathy, misunderstanding, and ignorance remain within the church. It will take some real work by both clergy and laity before divorced persons in the church can say, "My divorce was the best thing that ever happened to me."

II.
Loosening
the Tie that Binds:
Pain and Process

A tree is scarred by seasons of stress in its long effort of growth; but the leaves unfurl in the spring, and new life begins. All that is needed are sunlight, soil, and space. The tree of my life is brutally scarred—torn from its roots, homeless, and the leaves gone in the autumn of life. I hope that some day what I do now will be understood as the only way to preserve my sanity, protect my sons, and allow my wife's growth. Am I alone wise? I am terrified. But it has to be done.

These words were written in my journal ten years ago on a stormy day when I fled my marriage of twenty-three years and moved into an upstairs apartment. As I moved out, I took only my clothes, a television set, and my favorite Van Gogh—a picture of the artist's lonely room in Arles. I had begun a journey more demanding than I ever imagined. The long years of bitterness and conflict, endless sessions with therapists, and trial separations had ended. The break had come. I was thrust like a newborn babe into an existence far more uncharted than any world I had known. Even now I wonder, did it really happen? Or did I imagine it all?

Ronald D. Laing speaks of madness as a voyage of discovery in which people go through certain socially misunderstood experiences to return to the "normal" world with different perceptions of reality.[1] Through this exploration of inner time and space, growth occurs. Working through a divorce is a kind of madness, a journey into a strange world of loneliness, rejection, and pain that can either shatter people's sense of well-being or launch them into a new dimension of life. Little help was offered me during this agonizing time. It was not that people did not want to help—most of them just did not know how.

Sheila Kessler has said, "Getting divorced emotionally is akin to the way a sleepwalker feels when awakening at the edge of the roof, knowing little about the journey . . . or how to get down safely."[2] Everyone experiences divorce in different ways, but there is a common journey upon which all embark during the divorce proceedings and afterwards. Saying good-bye to old patterns is necessary before new life begins.

The Christian life affirms that ". . . the old has passed away, behold, the new has come (2 Cor. 5:17). The divorce process seems to follow certain stages, although not always in the same sequence. Like all human voyages, the journey of divorce is dynamic and fluid, but understanding the landmarks can help the church identify feelings of behavior common to those undergoing divorce. It is amazing that the emotional stages of divorce remain such an undiscussed subject. Many people are acquainted with the work of former priest Robert Kavanaugh, who in his book *Facing Death* has helped grieving people understand the normal stages of mourning the loss of a loved one. Elisabeth Kübler-Ross' stages of death and dying are well known. Roger Gould, Gail Sheehy, and Daniel Levinson have outlined predictable midlife crises, which are familiarly discussed. Unfortunately, however, most church members and religious leaders are woefully ignorant of the stages of the divorce process.

✱

STAGE

SEPARATION	MOURNING	IN-BETWEEN TIMES	RECONNECTION
		Experiences	
Emotional Yo-Yo	Depression	Identity Crisis	Survival as a Single
Euphoria/Distress	Remorse and Regret	Second Adolescence	Reestablishment in Community
Risk/Security			Possible Remarriage
		Major Tasks	
Reduce Separation Anxiety	Express and Resolve Emotions	Establish Stability Zones	Feel Secure as a Single Person
	Let Go of Past	Experience New Lifestyles	Develop New Friends
			Decide About Future Lifestyles

Why is it that some people adjust quickly to a marital separation, while others continue to experience unhappiness and pain for a long time? Why is it that for some separated/divorced people, grief over separation leaves deep scars which never seem to heal, while others find new life? Why is it that divorce catches some people off guard, leaving them wholly unprepared to deal with emotional upheaval and shock? The answers to these questions may be found in understanding the process of divorce, i.e., what happens to people as they uncouple. The church needs to become aware of this process, for ministry to the divorced can be effective only if it relates to the tasks of the present crisis.

Pastors need some awareness of the stages of divorce if they are to provide personal counseling and creative support for persons going through the divorce process. As the church has begun to respond to the dynamics of grief, so it needs to bring a theology of grace and truth to the crisis of divorce.

Stages of Divorce

Several authors have presented models outlining various phases of the divorce process. Sheila Kessler identifies seven stages of separation and divorce.[3] The first three, *disillusionment*, *erosion*, and *detachment*, all take place before physical separation. Spouses realize that their idealized image of their partner is unrealistic, and *disillusionment* results. *Erosion* sets in when such subtle means as avoidance and put-down behavior begin to destroy the relationship. In the first two stages, the marriage can be salvaged through renegotiation and/or marriage counseling. *Detachment*, however, is far more serious, for it marks the onset of apathy, and soon at least one partner begins to take steps toward independence. Once this stage is reached, it is highly unlikely that the marriage can be saved without therapy. *Physical separation*, the fourth stage, is the most traumatic, characterized by rapid mood swings from severe depression and anxiety to relief and bursts of energy. *Mourning* occurs when one realizes that the relationship has died, and people express the same emotions (anger, depression, helplessness) as those who lose a spouse by death. In *second adolescence*, the grown-up adolescent tests new limits in relationships and actions, examines and re-defines values, and selects new goals more consistent with the emerging self. The final stage, *hard work*, finds persons gaining new control over their lives, exhibiting renewed vitality and self-confidence. These stages are not meant to be chronological, since they may overlap and can be experienced in a different order. How long does each one last? A stage might go on for months, years, or a lifetime, depending on the person involved. Every person has an individual timetable based on his or her desire to move into new experiences.

Paul Bohannan outlines six "stations" in the divorce process. The first is *emotional divorce*, which centers on the problems of the deteriorating marriage. The second stage, *legal divorce*, refers to the changed legal status and new rights and responsibilities. The third station is *economic divorce*, marked by property settlements and economic reassignments. *Coparental divorce* is the fourth station, which concerns custody, single parenting, and visitation rights. The fifth station is *community divorce*, in which divorced persons begin a new life by seeking friends and relationships, often among others who are divorced. The final stage is the *psychic divorce*, when the person reorients his or her life.[4]

Donald J. Froiland and Thomas L. Hozman view divorce as a process of grief and relate the experience to the five stages of death and dying delineated by Elisabeth Kübler-Ross.[5] *Denial* that the marriage is beginning to disintegrate is followed by outbursts of *anger* and *bargaining* in attempts to preserve the dying relationship. Sadness and pessimism then combine to produce *depression*, which is finally resolved by *acceptance* and reorientation.

Abigail Trafford believes that the stages of divorce echo the three phases of human consciousness envisioned by the philosopher Kierkegaard in his *Courage to Live*.[6] The first level of response to divorce is the *hummingbird phase*, roughly equivalent to Kierkegaard's "aesthetic stage." During this stage, divorced persons refuse to face facts, and they flit from romance to romance or job to job. They avoid confronting the pain and anxiety of divorce by fluttering around as fast as possible. The second stage is *foundering*, analogous to Kierkegaard's "ethical or moral stage." This is the height of "crazy time" in divorce; people get stuck in their despair and pain. Trafford claims that "The danger is that some people never get beyond this level of psychological growth. They seem to give up life in despair and cynical resignation."[7] Next is the *phoenix stage*, the equivalent of Kierkegaard's "religious stage," which brings the person new control, confidence, and freedom from the past.

Although each of these theories has its merits, none captures succinctly and thoroughly the stages of divorce. For example, Froiland and Hozman depend too much on divorce as a dying experience and neglect other aspects of the divorce process. Kessler's stages focus too much on the intitial phases of the divorce journey and not enough on the redirection of life beyond divorce.

I discovered four major stages as I worked through my own separation and divorce and helped divorced people through their process. The first stage is *Separation*, which focuses on surviving the intial separation distress. When the reality of separation occurs, stage two, *Mourning*, begins, when divorced people must learn to grieve and then let go of the past. The third stage is *In-between Times*, the gray limbo between a past that is gone and the uncertain future. During this stage a new identity must be formed through hard work before the final stage, *Reconnection*, takes place, during which one feels a new wholeness and establishes a life beyond divorce.

In each stage of the divorce process, the individual has certain major tasks which need to be dealt with if he or she is to grow through divorce. The church needs to be aware of how these needs can be met.

Stage One: Separation

The moment that a spouse leaves—or is left—initiates an ordeal of anxiety, loneliness, and panic which has been described as separation anxiety. Unexpected mood swings occur and may continue for weeks or months. This emotional yo-yo finds the separated person alternating between feelings of euphoria and anxiety. For either brief or extended intervals there is a feeling of relief or joy that the conflict is over and the bitterness at an end. Some describe this feeling as "walking on air." Separating from a destructive marriage brings sudden outbursts of energy and a new zest for living. A forty-year-old woman described her experience this way:

> For a few hours last night I couldn't sleep replaying the old scenario of our marriage and divorce. I finally got dressed and went out into the night. I walked for hours and felt a strange joy. I had gotten through the night. It was all right. It was going to be all right.

However, relief and joy are soon replaced by anxiety, extreme loneliness, and fear of the unknown.

Robert S. Weiss gives this description of separation anxiety:

> It is marked by a focusing of attention on the lost figure, together with intense discomfort because of that figure's inaccessibility. There is likely to be unhappiness stemming from feelings of desolation. There may also be apprehensiveness, anxiety, or panic.[8]

The separated person begins to wonder if he or she really did make the right decision. Sitting in an unfamiliar apartment or deserted home, the person may magnify the former spouse's virtues and minimize the vices. That long-held identity with another person—such a major part of the self—is gone. It would be easier, one reasons, to go back. Certainly, going back would revive a semblance of togetherness, but soon the basic separateness would return, and the hard realization would hit: there is *no* going back.

An integral part of this separation anxiety is the terrible loneliness. Numerous studies have suggested that only a minority of those who are newly separated fail to be affected by it, and that even those who clearly looked forward to the end of their marriage find the initial loneliness of separation extremely painful.[9] One recently separated man described the especial difficulty of his first Christmas after separation:

What fool ever made separated persons go through Christmas? If anyone had ever told me how hard it is for separated people on Christmas Eve, I wouldn't have believed them. I had to be a visitor in my own home, a Santa Claus who returned to an empty apartment. I suddenly realized it was the first time in forty-five years that I didn't have a Christmas tree. If I can just make it through this Christmas, I might survive.

Separated people react in different ways to this anxiety. Some try to block out the pain. Feeling rootless and at loose ends, they try to stay busy with social engagements, although some of the activities may not even be pleasurable. Coming, going, doing become dominant. If I am too busy to think about the pain, I can't be hurt by it, they suppose. This "butterfly existence" finds them flitting from one party or engagement to another, often hardly aware of what they are doing. Separated men who are still trapped in the machismo image often refuse to admit they have any problems, and they either wallow in their solitude or crowd their schedules with endless activities. Some separated people begin a frantic search for another person and think that by finding a new partner they can resolve their anxiety. Such relationships, however, usually prove fleeting. At length, the truth dawns that the separation is real and cannot be denied. At the end of this stage the shock of what has happened gradually disappears. The marriage *is* over. Mourning has begun.

Stage Two: Mourning

A lot of people are caught off guard by the deep sadness and grief that follow separation. Divorce is a small death in this instance, but unlike a time of physical death it is an occasion which meets with others' rejection, not their acceptance or support. Paul Bohannan speaks of the reversal of the courtship process in divorce. Marriage means that one has been rewarded by being chosen by someone else. Divorce means that one has been rejected, and "It punishes almost as much as the engagement and wedding are rewarding."[10] It is not only rejection by the former spouse that causes pain, but also lack of support from others. Sometimes there is no one to rely on. Friends may have good intentions but few supportive skills. Most do not know whether to offer sympathy or congratulations; "I'm sorry" just does not mean very much. Furthermore, there is no service or ritual in which grief may be expressed openly and with dignity. An irony of our contemporary society is that at the very moment when it is becoming acceptable to express emotions at the death of a person, there is no acceptable ritual for such expression at the death of a marriage.

No one feels the need to apologize for the death of a spouse, but when a divorce occurs, both parties feel embarrassed and apologetic. I have never met anyone divorced who did not mourn and grieve for what might have been. A forty-five-year old woman poignantly described her mourning process:

> With the end of my marriage, I lost a part of me. We had shared a life together, and no matter how sensible the decision to separate, how can I forget the happy memories? I torture myself with thoughts of what I did wrong. My loneliness increases because I can't share my grief with anyone.

Recovery from the grief of divorce can be compared to recovery from surgery. The wound heals well if it gradually builds up healthy tissues, if the final scar covers such a good foundation that the healed wound does not hinder the person from living a normal life. A wound that does not heal is one that has an infection preventing complete recovery. In divorce, grief is an infection made up of unresolved feelings which may surface later on in the form of emotional or physical problems.

Two symptoms of the mourning process among divorced persons are depression and obsessive review. Depression is a "turtle time" when divorcing persons withdraw beneath their shells and try to escape. It is characterized by an exaggerated low mood, accompanied by feelings of helplessness and sadness.

Studies have shown that women reach the depths of depression faster than men, and that divorced women commit suicide three times more than married women. In a Beyond Divorce

Enrichment Group, a twenty-eight-year-old woman seemed euphoric about her recent divorce. Unlike many other group members, she claimed she had no problems but had found a new freedom. When the group was discussing depression, she loudly protested that *she* had never been depressed. But later on, after viewing a film on a mother's rejection of her divorcing daughter, she admitted:

> Shortly before I separated from my husband, I went through a period when I really did consider either suicide or disappearance. My parents just about died when they learned about the separation. I had been the "perfect child" and I think I would have fared better if I had robbed a bank. My choice then was either to kill myself, or my parents by the disgrace of my divorce.

One positive note is that the depression of divorced people is not as severe as that of people who cannot break unbearable ties in a marriage. The latter group feel irreparably hopeless and tend to be even more severely depressed than those who take steps to leave.[11]

Obsessive review involves repeated thoughts about the marriage and endless remorse over what went wrong. It is hard to let go of the past. Ties with another person are hard to sever. Like Gulliver tied to the ground with stakes and ropes by the Lilliputians, a separated person has thousands of ties binding him or her to the lost spouse. Many divorced people refuse to break those ties. They continue to live as if the relationship still exists. Willard Waller has observed that "the memory of a person may be dear after the person is dear no more." He tells of a man who looked for mail from his former spouse at all hours of the day, although he knew the letters would never come.[12] The experience of all separated people may not be as extreme as this, but many persons do become fixated on the past. In his novel *The Plague*, Albert Camus caught the sense of people unwilling to let go the past and robbing the present of meaning.

> Therefore they forced themselves never to think about the problematic day of escape, to cease looking to the future, and always to keep, so to speak, their eyes fixed on the ground at their

feet. . . . they drifted through life rather than lived, the prey of aimless days and sterile memories, like wandering shadows that could have acquired substance only by consenting to root themselves in the solid earth of their distress.[13]

One mourns not merely that divorce has ended the marriage, or that the former spouse is absent. The greatest grief is over the loss of the reinforcers of the married years—the comforts of home, financial security, happy holidays, and the warm feeling of someone to snuggle with in the dark night.

The hurt and pain must be experienced and lived out. Marcel Proust said, "We are healed of our suffering only by experiencing it." For some this means endless nights of tears or bouts with depression. Others, hasten the process with symbolic acts—moving to another community, refusing to answer hostile calls, finding a new job. One divorced man achieved his closure this way:

During the twilight, in a quiet outdoors, I threw my wedding ring into a lake. I knew than that my past was buried once and for all. It was time to go on with my life. The old had ended—the new was out there. The in-between times had begun.

Stages One and Two for Divorced Clergy

The pain of the first two stages of divorce is accentuated for divorced clergy. They experience certain unique traumas because of the exalted status given them by the congregation. Among the most common are accentuated guilt and failure, social rejection, victimization or martyr syndrome, and role diffusion. Pastors who divorce are downgraded and their guilt magnified by the functional guilt projected on them by congregations and colleagues who expect ministers to be models of success, especially in their home life. Some people, like the Lutheran minister Carl E. Braaten, have gone so far as to insist that ministers who separate ought to leave the ministry:

When a clergyperson gets a divorce, it ought to carry with it an automatic suspension from active service in the ministry. This will serve to minimize the public scandal and give time for the church and the pastor to determine whether, all things considered, he or she ought to be retained in the ordained ministry of the church. It is time for the church to withstand the infiltration of the secularized attitude which views divorce and remarriage on the par with buying and selling a house.[14]

Traditional interpretation of passages in the New Testament concerning divorce compounds this guilt and sense of failure.

When clergy divorce, there is little support and help available, especially during these crucial early stages. The clergyperson is perceived as different and strange, and only rarely does he or she receive the support of church governing bodies and peers. Except for rare encounters with other divorced clergy or supportive clergy, their experience is little different from that of divorced persons in the nineteenth century who were treated as moral lepers and discussed behind closed doors.

Caught in the bewildering web of polite silence or overt avoidance, many divorced clergy fall into the trap of becoming victims and martyrs. Studies have shown that many divorced persons feel so guilty that they unconsciously seek ways to punish themselves, such as living in uncomfortable surroundings or denying time for their children. Divorced clergy are no exception. They may crawl into "turtle time" and isolate themselves from the world, or they may join forces with others in the subculture of the formerly married who renounce the church for its censorious attitude. Their bitterness leads them to want no part of a church that wants no part of them. It is unfortunate that much of this bitterness may be projection, imagined rejection, and intentional isolation.

Another study has shown that for Protestant clergy, occupational norms and family roles are closely merged.[15] A failure at home means a failure in one's career. Those who have experienced the greatest negative impact on their careers have left the ministry altogether, victims of the rejection of a church which professes a gospel of love.

The poetry of divorced clergyman John C. Morgan expresses how the church so often fails divorced persons:

THE DIVORCE

In the Court:

I was found by the judge to be one
against whom no hideous crime could be proven,
save art and questions and being a liberal—
in Ohio, sins of the first order.
No reconciliation possible, said the lawyers;
no conciliation likely, said the social worker;
nothing worth saving here, said the judge.
"He is human. Nothing more need be said."
And the crowd roared.
Into this neutral place, where justice is ordinary
and judges eat oranges, peels on the floor,
the sentence was normal, typically so.
For life, mind you, for life.
For a life of remembering the eyes of the children,
judged as well though hardly to blame;
for the dreams strangled, as much by habit
as design.
In the cold type of the composing room
it was just another day,
another page of divorces, listed somewhere
on the obituary page.

The sentence was dying, there's no question about that.
The sentence was crying, there's no question about that.
The sentence was dying and crying and trying to live.
There's no question about that.

In the Pastor's Study

In the pastor's study the books on mercy
line the walls,
and texts on grief.
But he is cold.
Turn your deaf ear on me, cleric,
publish my sin in your book of failures;
your judging God
forgives no one, heals no one, frees no one

save the sinless who sit in your pews
shaking their heads in disbelief
and reciting the Lord's Prayer.
Turn your cold heart my way, cleric:
I am dying, can't you see?
"Take three Bible verses, and call me
in the morning."
And what if I die before then,
what if, like Jacob, I wrestle in the night
and refuse to let go?

The sentence was dying, there's no question about that.
The sentence was crying, there's no question about that.
The sentence was dying and crying and trying to live.
There's no question about that.[16]

Stage Three: In-between Times

For the person who has finally accepted the end of a marriage, a part of the self is lost. Mourning has gone on long enough. But the hardest time has just begun. The person now enters the empty space, that nameless limbo, between what was and what is yet to be. My brother John described this empty space vividly in a letter he wrote during his in-between times:

> I feel like climbing the walls. Suddenly, being alone, one realizes how much of the past has been filled with sounds and sights and how meaningless much of it has been. It is a period of my life in which the past has been closed and the future uncertain. Like the early Christians, I feel caught between the times—the old is gone, but nothing has come to take its place. I know, in the long run, that this is a growing period, but for now I feel alone, separated, and in some twilight zone where there are no longer any firm guideposts.

During this time, life becomes a daily struggle of forging some new kind of identity. Traditionally women have often linked the major portion of their identity to their marriage; they may continue to view themselves as part of a couple, with no personal identity outside the marriage. They may even suffer socially because of their presumed failure to keep their man. The societal myth of the gay divorcée out to seduce other women's husbands can lead to social ostracism of the divorced woman and her family. Linda, whose marriage broke up after fifteen years, told another divorced friend,

> You're darned right I feel betrayed. All those years I had supported him and his work. What he was doing was the important thing; we moved because of his job. So when he left I felt that my identity was so wrapped up in him that I find it hard to describe myself apart from him. Who am I, anyway?

Nor is it any easier for the man who realizes that he suddenly is brought back full circle to where he started, or worse. He has to give up everything he has worked for; he stands to lose his home, many of the things he loved, much of his property, a significant part of his income, and, worst of all, daily contact with his children. The divorced man may also be bewildered by practical matters. He may find it difficult to turn an apartment into a home. As men—and women—play the role of victim and exist in less than comfortable surroundings, they find solace in being martyrs. Ed, forty-five-year-old divorced man, found it difficult to leave his marriage, but now he is forging a new identity as a single man. He says,

> I left my marriage expecting a new life with unlimited freedom to "do my own thing." No responsibilities except to send the support payments every month. But it has not worked out that way. I have a place to sleep, a few friends, and my work. I guess I'll just have to be patient and hope things get better than this. Despite the pain, I am getting in touch with me.

In time, the stage which Sheila Kessler calls the "second adolescence" begins. The excitement of possible new adventures and risks recreates an almost adolescent state. Like Harry Haller in Hermann Hesse's *Steppenwolf*, the separated person is ready to leave the upstairs room of the past and explore the "magic theatre" of new possibilities. Some people even make radical changes in their lifestyle. Men grow beards, wear modish clothes, seek younger women, and join the swinging set— what some have termed "hip, Honda, and hirsute syndrome."[17]

Women, likewise, make sudden changes, like getting involved in numerous hobbies, joining women's groups, and frequenting nightclubs.

What one learns is that too much change can be as devastating as too much routine. Every person who separates tries to block out all the meaningless words that people speak at this moment of crisis. There may be some word, though, that lingers when all others are forgotten. The day after I separated a trusted friend came by my office and said,

> The one thing I want you to remember is "Don't make radical changes." So many people who separate feel they have to undergo major personality and behavior changes. I like you the way you are. It's okay to be you.

Now, years later, these words still remain as the most affirming comment I heard at the time of my separation. They made me realize that I was not some insane person or incorrigible beast who had abandoned his family. These words gave me courage to begin the trip through inner space and rebuild my life.

It is at this moment, when the glitter and glamor of the "butterfly" or "hummingbird" existence have waned, that it is essential to develop what Alvin Toffler has called "stability zones."[18] Such a zone might be a place of employment, a hobby, or even a familiar old car. One stability zone for divorced persons in the in-between time is the church. Although it may be difficult for separating couples to remain in the same church, some churches can provide security for the separated person.

Despite the bad press to the contrary, divorced people do not continue to be angry with God or desert the church. Many find that separation can become a moment of grace; the past is let go in repentance, and forgiveness becomes a reality. The empty space can become a time of renewal of faith in God, who provides a second chance to all broken people to build a new life of hope and joy. Often, divorced persons turn to the church during this time of transition and upheaval. Sad to say, however, the church does not always listen or respond. As one divorced person wrote,

I sit in my darkened apartment across the street from the church. The Christmas lights flash across my window. But there seems to be an invisible wall between me and that church. Will I ever go back? Or will I be in this "far country" forever?

The empty space can be a scary time for separated and divorced persons. Like the early Christians, they feel caught between a dead past and an unknown future. But as those early Christians lived to realize the presence and the power of the risen Lord, so separated persons can accept the pain of the past and face the challenge of the present. They begin to see that the empty space was not merely a time of terror and anxiety, but also a moment of new beginnings. They know that they have changed from being stymied by empty space to being strengthened through it. It is a necessary step toward growth and new directions. The light does come.

Stage Four: Reconnection

Reconnection, feeling whole again, gradually comes about as the divorced person begins to establish a new life. Reva S. Wiseman has said, "Acceptance of divorce implies that it no longer arouses a negative feeling to identify oneself as a divorced person."[19] One is satisfied with things as they are, and has learned what Alan Watts calls "the wisdom of insecurity." In my own experience, acceptance came when I realized that being single might well be my future state. Reconnection means becoming newly aware and beginning to care again. Jim, a thirty-seven-year-old teacher, played Russian roulette with his marriage for years before he finally left and established a new life. He described the reconnection stage when he wrote,

> It's strange—but the past seems so distant now, as if it never really happened. I know I used to be that person, but now I wonder how. The one solace I can find out of all this is that I have remained as true to myself as possible. I have accepted the privacy of my inner self as a reality which can never be totally revealed in another's presence.

Reconnection does not mean that the old problems and ghosts of the past will not return. Just when the tentative new life is beginning to feel safe, there may be a letter, a song on the radio, or a phone call that stirs up old feelings. Eventually, however, these reminders will have less power to evoke sadness and nostalgia. Nietzsche's words sum up the position of the reconnected person: "What does not kill me makes me stronger."[20]

In time, the moment arrives when divorced persons stop analyzing why the marriage "failed" and what they have learned from the divorce. Somehow, after the pain and questioning cease, a gentle acceptance follows, and the newly single person moves on with life, meeting each day with a fresh sense of grace and thanksgiving.

Roland der Pury compares marriage to a man and woman dancing together on a high tightrope. All couples have at least one fall, he says. Some break their necks when they tumble, but husbands and wives who have faith fall into each other's arms and climb back on the tightrope again. *Divorced people also dance precariously on a tightrope.* They have no partner to catch them when they fall. They do fall, and some break their necks. But they can also fall into a network of grace so that once again they can climb back and walk the fragile tightrope of life.

The question of new relationships and remarriage will be discussed later. The following guidelines for readiness for remarriage, proposed by clergyman Larry M. Correu, can also be clues as to whether reconnection has taken place:

> Am I squared away emotionally?
> Am I free from within?
> Am I able to trust others enough just yet?
> Am I taking my time so I will act free from pressures?
> What possible liabilities and assets am I carrying into another marriage?
> Where am I faith-wise in all this?
> Can I trust myself to love another and commit myself to that person?
> How do my offspring fit into the picture?[21]

Hermann Hesse experienced the trauma of divorce twice. At the age of fifty-four, he married a third time and discovered a mature relationship which lasted thirty-one years, the rest of his life. Hesse's 1914 poem "How Heavy the Days" reflects the unhappiness of separation from a dying marriage:

How heavy the days are.
There's not a fire that can warm me,
Not a sun to laugh with me,
Everything bare,
Everything cold and merciless,
And even the beloved, clear
Stars look desolately down,
Since I learned in my heart that
Love can die.[22]

Completely different is the poem called "Stages," which Hesse wrote in 1941 when he was full of the hope and joy that his third marriage had brought him:

As every flower fades and as all youth
Departs, so life at every stage,
So every virtue, so our grasp of truth,
Blooms in its day and may not last forever.
Since life may summon us at every age
Be ready, heart, for parting, new endeavor,
Be ready bravely and without remorse
To find new light that old ties cannot give.
In all beginnings dwells a magic force
For guarding us and helping us to live.[23]

The strange journey of divorce, which stretches from separation to reconnection, moves from "learning in one's heart that love can die" to "finding new light that old ties cannot give." A thirty-year-old woman in a church-supported divorce group envisioned her divorce as a crippling handicap that she would have to overcome slowly and painfully:

I sit here in my wheelchair watching the world pass me by. My mobility is now limited. Two years ago my world was shattered just as if the A-bomb of Hiroshima had been dropped on it. I did not die but my life will never be the same again. Invisible handicaps are the most devastating kind, and I know rehabilitation has been painful; the first few steps so uncertain, others picked me up when I fell as I tore down ramps and learned to laugh again. My wheelchair is not chrome and steel, but the stigma of divorce. My methods of survival are not tried, nor true. But I'm using sunsets, roses, and rainbows. I'm starting over.

There are no glib answers to the complicated problems of separation and divorce. However, many divorced people have used their experience to begin a new life, one that accepts the pain of the past, the challenges of the present, and the opportunities of the future.

III.
"'Tis All in Pieces":
The Need for
a Christian Theology
of Divorce

Almost everyone has worked on a jigsaw puzzle. It takes a lot of patience and persistence to get all the pieces together until the picture finally emerges. All the pieces of a Christian theology of divorce are present, but they are still unrelated and, in some sectors of the church, unknown. Although the vast number of divorced and remarried people in the church makes such a theology imperative, most church members cling to old ideas about the church and divorce. Ask average church members what Jesus said about divorce, and they'll stammer that they don't know, or mutter something about how Jesus was opposed to divorce except for adultery. Many church members still think the church teaches that divorce is an unforgivable sin for which there is no final redemption.

Even some of the more liberal restatements of old, rigid policies of mainline Protestant churches about divorce and remarriage have been disregarded in light of an evangelical backlash, or strangely lost in the shuffle. The church, therefore, still treats divorced persons with a strange inconsistency. At times, its acceptance is quick and almost too glib. At other times, polite silence or overt condemnation makes divorced persons feel unwanted and unwelcome. A crucial need exists for the church to make a Christian theology of divorce clear both to its divorced members and to those never divorced.

Evidences of the Need

As we recognize the large number of people divorcing in our time, we discover the need for a fresh theological understanding of divorce. Divorced persons still carry the baggage of shame and guilt from a religious frame of reference and often find these feelings reinforced by the prejudices of legalistic Christians. Most of these feelings stem from an outdated theology that condemns Christians who divorce and denies that divorce can be a redemptive experience. Many honest, devout Christians who divorce are no longer willing to accept a theology which states that the only "Christian" response to a destructive marriage is either to be reconciled to one's spouse or to remain permanently in an unmarried state.

The Roman Catholic Church has begun to address the injustices done to divorced/remarried Catholics. This is especially striking in light of the theological position which the Roman Church has taken on marriage. Its historic position has been that marriage is indissoluble; however, in recent developments the church has gradually evolved a position which recognizes degrees of indissolubility. Some observers date the beginning of the modern Divorced Catholics Movement in this country to the work of Monsignor Stephen J. Kelleher, who argued that Catholics whose marriage had failed had the right to a new church marriage, once they had recovered from the effects of the divorce. The start of his struggle for the rights of Catholics to divorce can be dated from 1968, with the publication of an article in the Jesuit periodical, *America*.[1] In this article, Kelleher called for an end to the Marriage Tribunal, which grants annulments. He opposed the "Good Conscience" Solution as token acceptance, and called for the "Welcome Home" solution which acknowledged the right of Roman Catholics to remarry in the church and to receive Holy Communion publicly. Later he went so far as to state that "There are many, many instances where the Church should encourage persons to obtain divorces."[2] Others in the Roman Church have joined this struggle and provided genuine ministry to separated, divorced, and remarried Catholics in America.[3] It may well be that the Roman Catholics will point the way for Protestants in this regard.

Despite the claim of the church that *all* sins are forgiven, divorce remains the unforgivable sin. It is incongruous that the church can forgive murderers, rapists, and drug addicts and seek their restoration, and yet cast stones at divorced persons. This hardline stance denies the biblical truth that "All have sinned and fall short of the glory of God" (Rom. 3:23). Les Woodson has well said,

> There is no justifiable reason for isolating divorce and/or remarriage from the rest of condemnations as if one somehow is worse than the others. . . . and what right do we have to label divorce as being more permanently contaminating than other sins?[4]

It is a strange anomaly of Christian history that the church has constantly recognized the need to relativize almost every other ethical demand of Jesus (i.e., don't be angry; be perfect; love your enemies) but has been *literal* only in its reading on divorce. Only recently, the Australian Anglican Synod has taken the stand that the remarriage of divorced persons, other than those who are innocent victims of adultery, contravenes ecclesiastical law.[5] This is a reversal of the Family Law Act of 1976, where clergy accepted the decision of secular law about guilt and innocence in actions involving adultery. It means that clergy who officiate at such weddings are probably acting in violation of church law. This is another example of the evangelical backlash, and confirms the belief of many divorced Christians that the church speaks with a forked tongue when it comes to real acceptance and forgiveness of divorced persons.

There now exist a growing number of divorced/remarried church members. What about their place in the church? When the goodness of the new marriage cannot be denied, when the obvious healing of old hurts cannot be dismissed, how can the church maintain its existing theology of divorce? No doubt some church members are embarrassed, if not offended, by the genuineness of such persons' new commitment and the positive witness of their reconciled family life. Are such folk merely to be endured as "weeds among the wheat" (Matt. 13:25), growing side by side with traditional married couples? The polite embarrassment that church members feel in the presence of divorced persons was apparent when one dear lady introduced me to a Sunday school class as a "widower" although she *knew* I was divorced. Even when the church members remarry, they are stereotyped and considered less "normal" than "nice" Christians whose marriages have remained intact. A Christian theology of divorce must speak to Christian remarrieds, whose number will increase even more dramatically by 1990.

Clergy have always had problems deciding what to do with people who seek remarriage, especially those who are members of the church. Strange ambiguities remain, despite some clear guidelines in most official church standards. Some clergy still refuse to remarry divorced persons, while others become "a marrying parson," remarrying everyone and anyone for a fee. Some ministers will leave the problem of divorced persons alone, much the same way they may leave untouched other complicated difficulties in the church. However, the situation becomes serious for a minister whose church gives him or her the responsibility of deciding whether or not to remarry divorced persons. There seems to be no commonly agreed-upon Christian answer to the question. Trying to determine who is the "guilty" or "innocent" party in the divorce is "straining out a gnat and swallowing a camel" (Matt. 23:24). A Christian theology of divorce and remarriage would clarify the question and provide some guidelines for clergy who increasingly are being confronted with this issue.

For these reasons it is crucial that such a theology be clearly stated. Robert E. Elliott has succinctly stated the task facing the church as

> . . . to mobilize a pastoral theology of divorce to assist on at least two levels: The first is to help persons in responsible decision-making about divorce itself. The second is to help persons in the crisis of the divorce process to respond to the redemptive possibilities therein.[6]

What Jesus Is Accused of Saying About Divorce and Remarriage

In almost every divorce group I have led, some person invariably raises the question of what Jesus really said about divorce and remarriage. Did he actually say that all divorce is a sin, that people who remarry unless there has been adultery are themselves guilty of adultery? The situation is complicated by the fact that it is possible to draw more than one interpretation from Jesus' teachings on the subject of divorce and remarriage. Nelson Manfred Blake offers a number of options:

(1) Christ taught the indissolubility of marriage and forbade all divorce.
(2) He allowed divorce, but only to the husband, and only for one cause, adultery.
(3) He allowed divorce for adultery to both husband and wife.
(4) Neither party to a divorce may marry again while his [or her] former mate is still alive. To do so is adultery.
(5) The innocent party may remarry, but not the guilty.
(6) Both parties may remarry, after sincere repentance.
(7) Adultery means only one thing, the sexual intercourse of a married person with someone other than the husband or wife.
(8) Adultery is a symbolic word, standing for any sin that violates the marriage contract.[7]

Many attempts have been made to explain and reconcile the variant words of Jesus about divorce in the gospels, but with very little success, and one must beware of dogmatic statements about what Jesus really said on the subject. The fact that Matthew adds the "exception clause" to cope with pastoral problems in the early church shows how difficult it is to know what Jesus actually said and what the gospel writers added to accommodate his teachings to their own situations. However, serious questions need to be raised about making the literal view of "no divorce except for sexual adultery" the explicit teaching of Jesus. Charles C. Ryrie, an evangelical scholar, takes a hardline approach and bases it on Jesus' teaching:

> Even if immorality occurs, forgiveness and reconciliation are the goals, not divorce. Even if a legal divorce should occur, the "one flesh" relationship cannot be severed and that is why remarriage is disallowed. . . . Doctrine must never be compromised by cases; cases should always conform to doctrine.[8]

However, the words of Jesus in the Synoptic Gospels about divorce and remarriage are far more complex than this simplistic interpretation implies; the excellent book by Myrna and Robert Kysar, *The Asundered*,[9] analyzes these passages in detail. Any consideration of Jesus' teachings on divorce should take into account the following important points.

(1) The priority of Mark's account

Most New Testament scholars believe that Mark was the original text, and view Matthew's alterations as evidence of his editorial activity in relating the message to a different context. William V. Arnold has said, "Many scholars feel that Matthew's account represents a mellowing that was going on in the early church. Apparently the church began to wrestle with the realism of adhering to an absolute position as stated in Mark.[10] Mark wrote his Gospel for a Graeco-Roman audience where divorce was permissible for women as well as men. Thus Mark, unlike Matthew, was aware that women could secure a divorce (Mark 10:12).[11] As Mark clearly states, Jesus taught that God's intention is for people to remain married. The original and earliest word of Jesus on marriage was "What therefore God has joined together, let no[t] man put asunder" (Mark 10:8).

Mark places Jesus' sayings on divorce in the context of a

dispute over the authority of the law. The questioners of Jesus hoped to trap him into contradicting the law, which permitted divorce on grounds of men's "hardness of heart." In response, Jesus asserts God's greater intention in creation and states that this is a prior and far greater authority than the permission given through the law for divorce. Here Jesus is holding in theological tension the divine intention for indissoluble marriage and the necessity for divorce resulting from "hardness of heart."

(2) Matthew's unique context

In order to understand the way Matthew changes and adapts Jesus' words (as recorded in Mark) to his own milieu, one must remember two things: (1) there was a current, ongoing rabbinic controversy over the meaning of Moses' words about divorce, and (2) first-century Pharisaism was extremely chauvinistic and denied women the right to divorce their husbands. In the days of Jesus the rabbinic schools of Shammai and Hillel quibbled over the meaning of Moses' statement that a man can divorce his wife "because he has found some indecency in her" (Deut. 24:1). Rabbi Hillel and his followers stressed the vague word *dabar* ("thing") and came to the conclusion that practically anything was sufficient grounds for divorce. A man could divorce his wife at the drop of a hat if he didn't like her looks, if she burned the roast, or even if she was merely responsible for some early Hebrew equivalent of "ring around the collar." All the man had to do was write out a bill of divorce, and the separation was quite legal. Certain passages in the Old Testament classify women merely as property, along with cattle and land (e.g., Gen. 21:14; Jer. 6:12). A possible example of a certificate of divorce is the succinct wording in Hosea 2:2: "She is not my wife, I am not her husband."

Divorce was that simple for the man. For the women there were no rights, no court-appointed lawyers, no right of appeal. The School of Shammai stressed the word *erwat* ("shame") and demanded that the reason for divorce be a serious one, something that involved shame, such as adultery. To stress the point, the School of Shammai would even invert the phrase of Deuteronomy 24:1 to read *debar erwat*, "the thing of shame." Notice that in the Matthean account when the Pharisees asked Jesus if it was lawful for a man to divorce his wife, Jesus went back to God's original intention. He refused to take sides in the issue. Matthew, however, writing for the Jewish Christians at Antioch who sided with the Shammai, added the "exception clause." Thinking that the church had the power to make such decisions (Matt. 18:18), Matthew inserted the clause to bring Jesus' teachings in line with the practices of the Palestinian church.

A good example of one of the many interpretations of Jesus' words about divorce and remarriage occurs in a recent article by Keith Rayner.[12] He claims that Jesus' questioners assumed that any action permitted by the law was in accordance with God's will and therefore morally right. Jesus makes it clear, though, that merely keeping within the letter of the law does not constitute a moral action.

> For a man to divorce his wife *in order* to marry another woman has the character of adultery (just as to lust on her in his heart has). . . . If this understanding is correct, this is not a blanket statement that every marriage after divorce is adulterous. What is adulterous is the act of breaking up one marriage in order to marry someone else.[13]

Thus Rayner believes that Jesus does not condemn all remarriages, since Jesus' words do not refer to people who divorce with no intention of remarrying and who subsequently marry someone who was in no way connected with the breakdown of the former marriage.

Rayner even finds in the words of Jesus justification for remarriage, surely a shift from the way remarriage is traditionally condemned in the name of Jesus. According to Rayner, the words that conclude Jesus' discussion of marriage and divorce in Matthew 19:3–9—"it is not expedient to marry"—present a precept which not all men could receive. Celibacy is a vocation to which not all are called, especially divorced persons. "The possibility is not ruled out that it may be God's positive will for some in this situation to marry again. In such cases it would be right for the Church to bless the new union."[14]

Rayner's view would have Jesus condemning not all remarriages after divorce (even when no adultery is involved), but only those which find the person breaking up one marriage to marry someone else. People who truly repent and seek God's grace to make of the new marriage a Christian union should be blessed by the church.

The Radical Life-giving Teaching of Jesus

We know for sure that Jesus protected the rights of women. Jewish law gave men dominance in marital affairs, while women were treated as property to be used (and discarded) at will. Obviously, Jesus would oppose an institution of divorce in which women were always the losers! The vast majority of women in the first century found marriage their only vocation, and to be divorced was not only a personal disgrace, but a social disaster. Hillel's philosophy had to be stopped if women's rights were to be protected. *Thus Jesus' resistance to divorce may have been more directed at redressing this abuse than at rejecting the principle itself.*

Still, Mark's Gospel presents the problem of Jesus' absolute demand that all marriages be unbroken. Dwight Hervey Small tries to solve this dilemma with his view that the radical ethics of Jesus cannot be applied to our sinful age. He suggests that there are three ages of ethical principles: (1) The Mosaic period of the Old Testament, in which God allowed divorce because of the hardness of men's hearts; (2) The Future Kingdom Period, in which righteousness will be perfectly fulfilled and divorce will not exist; and (3) the Interim Church Period, the present, which is under grace, not law.[15]

Small further concludes that Christ's ban on divorce and on remarriage except with the grounds of adultery is a commandment for the Future Kingdom Period and therefore invalid for the Interim Period in which we now live. Marriage should be honored, but the radical demand of Jesus cannot be applied to this age. The Christian who fails nevertheless lives under grace, and the forgiveness of God enables him or her to begin again, even in a new marriage.

No doubt this interpretation would relieve a lot of guilt in the minds of Christians who remarry. It does seem to hold tight to the literal words of Jesus without binding Christians to a destructive marriage. But I believe Christ's words are to be taken seriously for this age, not reserved for some "Future Kingdom." The tension between law and grace is clear. God demands that marriages last throughout life, but if Moses allowed for divorce caused by hardness of heart, surely Jesus, in whom is the fullness of grace and truth (John 1:17) would be compassionate to those whose marriages end. We can say with certainty only that Jesus was reaffirming the sanctity and importance of marriage (without trying to legislate when and where it might be dissolved) and in that context was championing the cause of women. The church has often fallen into a new legalism by making Jesus' words about divorce into juridical principles which Jesus never intended. Theologian John B. Cobb, Jr., has well said, "The New Testament does not lay down a new set of laws to replace the old. When it is read in that light it becomes the most repressive law ever promulgated, capable only of producing guilt and despair."[16] How tragic that the compassion of Christ for all fallen sinners should be kept from divorced persons because of such legalism! It seems hardly believable that the Jesus who forgave the woman "caught in the act of adultery" (John 8:1–11) would ever condemn those whose marriages end in divorce.

Furthermore, if Jesus allowed for the breaking of honored traditions about the sabbath and other institutions to provide for healing, would he not also allow for marriages to be broken to provide for the liberation of persons? Other scholars argue that Christ's response to that situation ought not to be codified into universal law. Jesus always advocated love, not law, as the guideline for human behavior; we must seek to interpret the spirit of his teaching, not be bound by its letters. Christ's ideal of lifelong marriage must not become a millstone for all who fail. This new spirit seems to underlie the revised confession of the Presbyterian Church. After reiterating that Jesus' words about divorce in the Synoptic Gospels came in response to specific questions about divorce, the document says,

> In no sense does he [Jesus] deal with the troublesome "what ifs" that intrude into every contemporary discussion of marriage. "What if a particular marriage under consideration appears to have been ill-considered, an example of blind, youthful impulsiveness from the start, based, almost exclusively upon 'hardness of heart' rather than God's 'joining'?" "What if in the course of a marriage, the marriage relationship becomes fundamentally destructive to the partners (and/or their children), *then* what shape does God's gracious intention take?"[17]

This is not to deny that divorce is a tragedy or to assert that remarriage is always redemptive. It is to say that both law and grace, both penitence and forgiveness must be present in a Christian divorce. The statements of Jesus on the subject of marriage and divorce give marriage a position of the highest dignity. In regarding marriage as an indissoluble union and in placing husband and wife in a relationship of equality, Jesus went beyond both Jewish and pagan conceptions. It is difficult, however, to relate his teachings to the problem of divorce in the modern world, since he did not deal with particular issues of human failure in any given marriage. Such questions must be answered on the basis of the gospel as a whole, rather than on the proof of isolated, individual verses or phrases. Furthermore, Jesus did say, "When the Spirit of truth comes, he will guide you into all the truth" (John 16:13). Although we can never minimize Jesus' radical demand that marriage last throughout life, neither can we bypass his compassion for broken people. When the question of divorce involves both penitence and resolution to begin a new life, there is little doubt how Jesus would respond. The gospel as a whole is at stake here.

Some Individual Efforts

There have been some scattered efforts at stating a Christian theology of divorce. James G. Emerson, Jr., after studying various attitudes and actions of the church in regard to divorce and remarriage, tried to improve them by an approach which spoke to the needs of persons, rather than the need of the church to maintain the status quo. He believed that people contemplating remarriage carry a burden of guilt and need "realized forgiveness."[18] Realized forgiveness emphasizes the Christian view of time (*kairos*), which is not seen as clock time (*chronos*) but as an experience of fulfillment at the deepest level of life. All history is caught in "the uniqueness of Christ's love and forgiveness," so that time is to be viewed as "an experience of relationship." Marriage can die; realized forgiveness affirms this reality, but moves beyond it to forgiveness which frees persons from the sin of broken marriages.

In 1977 Robert F. Sinks proposed a theology of divorce based on situational ethics and claimed that divorce can be a responsible act, "a creative, positive and affirmative response, ethically justified as that option which best approximates fulfilling the Great Commandment in the midst of limited alternatives."[19] Sinks believed that divorce, at times, may be the appropriate response of love:

> If Jesus allowed for breaking the honored Sabbath laws so as to provide for healing or gleaning, though the ancient laws forbade these on the sacred day, would he not also allow for a suspension of the proscription against divorce if such were to liberate a person from the bondage of an intolerable marriage? If the Sabbath was "made for man, not man for the Sabbath" (Mark 2:27), does it not follow that marriage was made for humanity, rather than humanity for marriage?[20]

Persons come before institutions; if the health and well-being of persons collide with any marriage, then persons come first. Joseph Fletcher, an American Episcopalian clergyman, once said, "Getting a divorce is sometimes like David's eating the reserved Sacrament; it is what Christ would recommend."[21]

While Sinks admits that there are some divorces clearly arising from sinful and selfish motives, there are others, while resulting from the fallen nature of humanity, that are not specifically evil acts. Although the position of situational ethics does prevent a rigid, legalistic approach to divorce, it can also pervert love into a congenial sentimentalism that simply condones whatever we do. The historic Calvinist position about the pervasiveness of sin seems far more responsible. Condoning divorce by ignoring the words of Jesus, or resorting to overemphasis on personal needs, in no sense relieves one of responsibility for a broken marriage. Sinks stresses grace, but unfortunately he neglects truth.

Thomas M. Olshewsky has written a Christian theology of divorce which seems to effect a creative balance between grace and truth. He advocates letting go of the past in repentance and seeking new life in faithfulness and forgiveness. Supporting the view of marriage as a covenant, Olshewsky approaches divorce as a confrontation with the judgment of God but also as an opening to God's grace, thus retaining the balance. He chastises both the legalist and the libertine in their approaches to divorce. The legalist, according to Olshewsky, uses the "escape clause" in Matthew as a basis for self-justification. The libertine ignores the words of Jesus, claiming that these words are no longer relevant. "But for a Christian understanding of divorce, we must acknowledge the divorce as a failure to find in the marriage the fulfillment of God's promise. . . . and that we have been unfaithful to our commitment."[22] Olshewsky continues, "The Good News is that God's judgment is also God's grace. The same forgiving love that empowers us to acknowledge our sin of the past enables us to leave that past behind."[23] In Olshewsky's balance of law and grace, all the major themes of the Christian faith are linked with the experience of divorce. However, this theology of divorce fails to consider the role of the church as the community of faith and the question of how this theology can be communicated within the church.

Sandra Read Brown's recent work on divorce and remarriage reinforces the need for these considerations. Reflecting on the increasing incidence of clergy divorce and remarriage, Brown calls for a rethinking of the church's stance. What is needed is a theology that provides "a delicate balance beween truth and grace as opposed to a position of either condemning or condoning what is happening."[24] Brown's concept of "truth" means that the divorce and remarriage cannot be condoned or dismissed lightly, because breaking a sacred union does matter. Those whose first marriages have ended need to realize what they have done and assume responsibility for their part in the failure. Similarly, her concept of "grace" means that divorced and remarried persons should never be condemned: ". . . their marital failure or remarriage neither disqualifies them from the human race nor calls for them to be rejected for being sinful."[25]

Recently, T. Craig Weaver has written about a Niebuhrian view of divorce. He shows how Reinhold Niebuhr's theology in its realistic approach to humanity and to the kingdom of God provides a solid foundation of a Christian perspective on divorce. He concludes that "Divorce is always an acknowledgment of failure, but it is not always a sinful act in itself. Divorce may be sinful or it may be the lesser of sins and, therefore, the right thing to do. . . . in response to man's sinful failure in marriage, God is ready to forgive and bless new beginning, even remarriage, for anyone, upon his repentance."[26] Weaver further appeals to the church to be redemptive in its response to persons and families experiencing divorce, to help them return to the life of the church. "The church must be an advocate for the divorced, affirming their equality with others in the sight of God and prophetically critiquing social, cultural prejudices within and without the church."[27]

Official Church Restatements

The Roman Catholic Church has adopted more liberalized guidelines regarding divorce and remarriage. Although Roman Catholic law still holds that marriage is indissoluble, the church is becoming more flexible in its attitude toward annulments. A richer understanding of "pastoral clemency" toward divorcing persons, and a broader interpretation of annulments ("lack of due discretion," "incapacity to marry," and "antisocial or immature personality") point to continuing changes within the Roman Church.

Some mainline Protestant churches have revised their older positions on divorce and remarriage with liberalized statements. In the Protestant Episcopal Church, the right for remarriage was given from 1868 to 1946 only "to the innocent party in a civil divorce." In 1946, the Episcopal Church repudiated the exception for adultery, allowing remarriage only for nullity. The permission of the bishop was still required for a divorced church member to marry again, but the ambiguity of the formula prolonged the issue. The present Canons of the Episcopal Church allow for divorce and remarriage; although they contain no statement of grounds or of how often a person may divorce and still receive the blessing of the church, Canon 18, Sec. 2 (A) sets out procedures which are to be followed should a divorced person wish to remarry according to the rites of the church.[28]

Theologian Philip Turner believes that American Episcopalians have become too permissive on this issue, since the Canons allow for divorce and nullity with no specifications of acceptable grounds.[29] Turner claims that Canon 18 is too vague about grounds for divorce, stating that "Such a Babel produces further confusion, misunderstanding and anguish. It serves also to weaken further the teaching about permanence found in Canon 17."[30]

Turner would revise Canon 18, Section 1 in the following manner:

> It shall also be the duty of the minister to give instruction concerning the grounds upon which the church has allowed for divorce. These are an irretrievable breakdown of the marital union which renders impossible the mutual society of the couple or a grievous offense in violation of the marital vows, such as adultery, desertion, or prolonged ill-treatment.[31]

The law of the former Presbyterian Church, U.S.A., now united as the Presbyterian Church (USA), revised its stance on divorce and remarriage in 1953. Section 2 of its *Constitution* stated that "while the corruption of man may put asunder what God hath joined together, remarriage is grounded in the redemptive gospel of Christ which demands penitence for sin and the intention to form a Christian remarriage."[32]

The former Presbyterian Church, U.S. also revised its stance on the issue. An Ad Interim Committee of the Council of Christian Relations, headed by Donald G. Miller, examined the complexity of the problem, showed areas of agreement and disagreement, and then made a recommendation to revise the Confession of Faith to allow no exception for divorce, since the exception clause was not originally part of Jesus' teachings. Nothing could be resolved, so a new Ad Interim Committee, chaired by Ernest Trice Thompson, subsequently recommended a more liberal view. Prior to that time, the ruling of the church was that "only the innocent party" in case of desertion or adultery could remarry. This naïve interpretation of one person as "innocent" and the other as "guilty" overlooked mutual involvement in broken relationships, whatever the circumstances.

Amendments were made in 1958 both to the *Westminster Confession of Faith* and *The Book of Church Order*. In the historic Confession of Faith, paragraph XXVI, section 6 was amended to read,

> The remarriage of divorced persons may be sanctioned by the Church in keeping with the redemptive Gospel of Christ, when sufficient penitence for sin and failure is evident, and a firm purpose of and endeavor after Christian marriage is manifested.[33]

It is striking that 17 biblical passages were cited to sanction this more liberal position.[34] The 1958 General Assembly also changed its *Book of Church Order*, paragraph 376, to reflect a similar modification:

> . . . being mindful always of the infinite mercy of God and careful never to hold against any honest child of God a sin which God himself may have forgiven and put behind Him forever. In a word, in all cases where remarriage is sought, the minister's decision shall turn not so much on what the applicant has done but rather on what this person by God's grace has now become, and what, with God's help, he (or she) honestly intends and hopes to do in the future.[35]

These amendments were approved, but not without protest.[36]

The recently reunited Presbyterian Church (U.S.A.) adopted the Confession of Faith as part of its constitution and reaffirmed the liberalized view that "the proclamation of the gospel of reconciliation in Jesus Christ" blesses not only first marriages, but marriage after being divorced (*Directory for the Service of God*, S–5.0400).

The United Lutheran Church of America also revised its policy toward divorce. Since 1930, its rule had been to limit the right to remarriage to the innocent party, but in 1956 it voted to permit a new marriage where there was evidence of repentance. God in love accepts all sinners and deals with them according to their individual situations. Persons seeking remarriage must recognize their responsibility in the divorce, give evidence of repentance, forgive the former partner, promise to fulfill obligations to those involved in the former marriage, show evidence of Christian faith, and be prepared to undertake the responsibilities of a new marriage. Pastors and congregations were to base their decisions upon "the particular circumstances in each case."

In 1884, the Methodist Church added the following Rule to the Discipline:

> That no divorce shall be recognized as lawful by the Church exept for adultery. And no minister shall solemnize a marriage in any case where there is a divorced wife or husband living; but this rule shall not apply to the innocent party in a divorce for the cause of adultery, nor to divorced parties seeking to be reunited in marriage.[37]

Thus, the discipline of the Methodist Church did not allow Methodist ministers to remarry divorced persons whose former mates still lived, except in two cases. First, they were allowed to remarry the divorced couple to each other. Second, they were allowed to marry the innocent party. This law was modified in 1932 to permit the remarriage of the innocent party in cases where "the true cause for divorce was adultery, or other vicious conditions which through mental or physical cruelty or physical peril invalidated the marriage vow."[38] In 1964 this troublesome provision was dropped, and each minister was counseled to perform the remarriage of divorced persons when convinced that the divorced person is aware of the reasons for the failure of the marriage, that the person is preparing to make the new marriage truly Christian, and that sufficient time has elapsed for adequate preparation and counseling.[39] In 1976 the United Methodist Church took its most liberal stance on the issue by adopting the following statement, which was reaffirmed in 1980 and 1984:

> We assert the sanctity of the marriage covenent. . . . In marriages where the partners are, even after thoughtful consideration and counsel, estranged beyond reconciliation, we recognize divorce and the right of divorced persons to remarry, and express our concern for the needs of the children of such unions. To this end we encourage an active, accepting, and enabling commitment of the Church and our society to minister to the needs of divorced persons.[40]

Research indicates that, while many Baptists oppose divorce except in the case of adultery, there is no official Baptist position on divorce and remarriage because of the unique nature of Baptist polity, stressing as it does the autonomy and independence of each local congregation. There have been no official resolutions at recent Baptist Conventions on the subject of divorce and remarriage. In this regard, they are unlike other mainline Protestant churches.

In her article "Religion Comes to Terms with Divorce," *USA Today* writer Janis Johnson lists some of the changes taking place in churches and synagogues regarding divorce and remarriage:

> Removing religious impediments to divorce and remarriage.
> Paying more attention to premarital counseling, and helping the separated and divorced readjust afterward rather than ostracizing them.
> Implementing divorce services as an ending ritual, just as the wedding ceremony began the marriage.[41]

In conclusion, there remain two major approaches in the Christian church to the issue of divorce and remarriage. One approach maintains that marriage is permanent and that only physical death frees the surviving person from the binding commitment. Those who hold this belief base their claim on Paul's words in Ephesians 5:22–23 which make the marriage of a Christian man and woman a symbol of the indissoluble union between Christ and the church. Just as it is unthinkable, they allege, for Christ and the church to go their separate ways, so it is unthinkable for a man and a woman in a Christian marriage to part.

The other approach insists that it is inconsistent to move in such a literalistic, legalistic manner, that God, who joined man and woman together may also put them asunder. Divorce may then be the human acknowledgment of what God has already done; blessed by forgiveness and grace, divorced persons can be remarried within the church.

In the mid 1950s, the debate in the Presbyterian Church, U.S., typified this struggle. Among the church people who maintained the hardline approach to divorce and remarriage was Donald G. Miller, who said unequivocably that

> . . . in biblical terms, the effort to repair a damaged marriage by another one is considered adultery; for the reality of the former marriage still exists, even though it may have been woefully sinned against and violated in the extremest form. The way to repair it is not to undo it, and substitute another one for it, any more than God substituted another than Eve for Adam, or another Adam as his own child.[42]

Miller argued that the Mosaic permission of divorce was a concession to the hardness of men's hearts "in the time of ignorance" before the coming of Jesus. After Jesus and the resurrection, this concession became invalid. Linking marriage with God's unique acts in history, Miller said, "The dissolution of a Christian marriage therefore is as unthinkable as that Christ could be born again, suffer again, rise again. That having been done can neither be undone or redone."[43] Christians have no choice but to repair a ruptured marital relationship or to remain in it and bear the pain.

Ernest Trice Thompson, representing the liberal position, claimed that the present standards regarding divorce and remarriage were ". . . written for another day and are based on a legalistic interpretation of Scripture which we can no longer accept as valid."[44] He believed that the legalistic interpretation of

Scripture was unreasonable and was also contrary to the principle of Christian liberty so forcibly argued by Paul in his letter to the Galatians. Thompson maintained that the proposed changes in the Confession of Faith of the former Presbyterian Church, U.S., did not lower the standards of the church to meet the practices of the church, but raised the standards to our understanding of the mind of Christ. He said that

> As the Master Teacher, Jesus seems indeed to have set forth principles in such an extreme way that his disciples could not possibly take them as binding rules, but would be forced to seek for the underlying principle which, under the guidance of the Holy Spirit, they would be expected to apply to the problems of their own day.[45]

The Spirit did work among those who liberalized the church's statements on divorce and remarriage, but that same spirit has not yet filtered down to the person in the pew, or even to some clergy and church judicatories. Thompson's clear statement of Christian principles became the touchstone for the new Christian theology of divorce, a theology which balanced truth and grace with sensitivity, a theology we need to examine with greater detail.

> No man and woman can marry in hope, and fail in that endeavor, without receiving scars which follow them both through life, but the church, if it is truly representative of its Master, will be willing to forgive, and to restore those who fall, to aid their further attempts to build a Christian home, and to give them all possible support in this endeavor. It will allow God to take care of the inevitable consequences that ensue from the previous failure. The church itself is concerned primarily, not with what man has done in the past, but with what may become in the future with the help of Jesus Christ, in and through the church, which is his body.[46]

IV.
A Christian Theology of Divorce

In the seventeenth century the noted Puritan theologian and poet John Milton wrote movingly of the need of the Christian churches to reexamine their harsh stance on divorce.[1] Earlier, the sixteenth-century theologian Martin Bucer had also written about divorce, challenging his fellow Christian clergymen to reconsider some of their views.[2] Both Milton and Bucer, however, failed to influence the tide of Christian opinion on divorce.

Today, the advocates of a more liberal approach to divorce in the church appear to have won a pyrrhic victory. Even conservative theologian Lewis R. Smedes admits that "The struggle to outlaw divorce absolutely within the Christian community is over; we have lost that struggle. And we will not contain the epidemic of divorces in society and church by continuing it."[3]

Even though many churches are adopting a more liberal attitude toward divorce, it takes time for individual congregations to change. Most divorced people are still unclear about how the church responds to them. Some church members gloss over their problems with simple naïveté, while others seem to say, "If you were a Christian, you would never have gotten a divorce." The result is that most divorced persons in the church feel either exonerated, needing no forgiveness, or extremely wicked, unworthy to receive the forgiveness of the church. As William H. Willimon has said, "I fear that, in our admirable desire to deal with divorced and divorcing persons in a more humane way, we have offered them cheap grace in place of the gospel, vague and permissive generalities in place of an honest confrontation with the challenge of marriage and the tragedy of divorce."[4] A Christian theology of divorce, which offers a creative balance between grace and truth, has yet to be effectively communicated to divorced persons.

Based on a Theology of Marriage

Marriage involves a covenant relationship between husband and wife, an answer to the primal loneliness of which Genesis speaks: "It is not good that man [woman] should be alone; I will make . . . a helper fit for him [her]" (Gen. 2:18). The covenant between husband and wife is similar to that between God and people. The marriage analogy in Hosea of the covenant between God and Israel makes this clear. Like the covenant, marriage is intended primarily for the healing of brokenness and the providing of intimacy throughout life. The terms of the covenant are not spelled out as agreements about certain conditions, as they are in a contract. A covenant is a relationship that both persons enter with mutual love and respect. On the basis of that love and respect, they commit themselves to each other "till death do us part." In the covenant of marriage, as in the covenants of the Bible, the following elements are present:

(1) the initiative of love which creates the relationship;
(2) the oath or vow of consent;

(3) the loyal love which sustains the covenant;
(4) the note of sacrifice.

This covenant of marriage is entered into by Christians in the presence of God and the community of faith. God is called upon to bless the marriage, a reminder that only the Creator's grace fulfills the covenant:

> Make their life together a sign of Christ's love to this sinful and broken world, that unity may overcome estrangement, forgiveness heal guilt, and joy conquer despair.[5]

For every Christian divorce, there was first of all a Christian marriage. Both partners began the marriage with every good intention of being "mutually helpful" to each other and keeping the covenant with loyal love.

Perceived as a Dying Experience

A Christian theology of divorce necessitates seeing divorce as a dying experience. Divorce closely resembles the dying process, and the passages through which individuals move involve loss and reestablishment. However, the dying involved in a divorce is never a single experience, but one interwoven with a web of other relationships—with oneself, with significant others, and with life itself. Both marriage and divorce are dying experiences. Marriage involves death to the dependency of childhood, and to the single life. Divorce, however, is a major dying experience, because along with adaptation and change, it involves loss and sorrow. Jim, who had been married for fifteen years before his divorce, describes his experience this way:

> I really thought my life had ended. Oh, I knew I would survive, but never as the same person as before. There was so much I had to let go of: my wife, my children, my home—all those parts of my experience I had claimed for so long. I am not sure how I found the strength to go on—but I did. I know I am stronger for having done so.

Divorce is another small death along life's journey. Each of us begins the journey at the moment of birth and ends it with death. But between these two points we are interrupted by the small deaths which touch the roots of our being. Robert Farrar Capon describes the dying that takes place in divorce:

> The rule, in remarriage as elsewhere, is: the first one to die wins. Is your former husband still lively in his insistence that the two of you are unreconciled? Does your former wife invite you constantly still to live at odds? If they do, that is sad for them. But if you believe that in God's grip all those indispositions are over—and that they are over *now*, because his hands hold all of us now—then you can lay hold of what he holds any time you're willing to die.[6]

Working through a divorce means experiencing a small death with all the pain that it brings. Because divorce is closely similar to the process of bereavement, all of the emotions that go with the loss of a loved one are often present during a divorce. Spiritual death is as real as physical death, and divorce is a symbol that marriage has died at the heart.

Viewing divorce as a dying experience is crucial to a Christian theology of divorce because it insists that there was "a real marriage" in the first place. When divorce occurs, it is neither helpful nor healthy to quibble over whether there ever was a valid marriage. John Milton believed that a marriage might turn out not to have been a real marriage all along; what he called divorce was really annulment. His unhappy marriage to Mary Powell, a disastrous mismatch, no doubt influenced his views. It was within the first year of Milton's marriage that his first divorce pamphlet appeared. Although Milton's theory might bring relief to people who divorce, it begs the question. A theology of divorce has to deal with real divorce. If vows were exchanged in freedom and with the intention to keep the covenant, there has been a real marriage, however unsatisfactory that marriage might have been. New life cannot emerge after divorce unless there is the death of the old marriage.

Recently, Philip Turner has shown how "irretrievable breakdown" is grounds for divorce. When a marriage dies and the relationship cannot be restored, the loving thing to do is let the other person go. As Turner says,

> Viewed in such a manner, in a case of irretrievable breakdown, the vow to show care might require loosing rather than binding one's

partner. In such an extreme situation, divorce might be the only way left to fulfill one's original vow. . . . Thus, divorce on the grounds of irretrievable breakdown may be seen as analogous to that shift in treatment sometimes appropriate in the care of the dying. There is often a point where one ceases to attempt to cure or to strive for the prolongation of life. One simply makes the person comfortable and allows them to die. Appropriate care in some instances means letting go. Allowing another to die might be the only way left for a doctor to fulfill his or her oath. Divorce, involving an irretrievable breakdown or *moral death* might be a precisely analogous case.[7]

Divorce as Breaking the Covenant: Adultery as Relational Failure

Divorce means that both partners have been unfaithful to the covenant relationship. It matters little how naïve or immature the couple was when the covenant was first established; both must face the responsibility of not keeping the covenant. There are no "innocent" or "guilty" parties in a Christian divorce. My grandfather, G. Campbell Morgan tried to skirt this issue this way:

> I have always taken the position of refusing to perform the marriage ceremony in the case of the guilty party, but not in the case of the innocent. In their case, the infidelity of the guilty sets them entirely free.[8]

Such a simplistic solution will not work. Those who are honest will recognize that only rarely is one spouse clearly guilty and the other absolutely innocent. It may be true that one had an affair and the other was sexually faithful, but the "innocent" spouse may have been so rejecting and cold that the "guilty" partner felt forced to find love and reaffirmation outside marriage. Until both parties acknowledge their responsibility in breaking the covenant, there is no possibility of a Christian divorce. Couples must painfully admit that once there was a real marriage which ended at some point and ceased to be authentic. Two persons broke the covenant; two persons committed adultery. *Here, adultery is defined as relational failure.* Most people still view adultery as sexual faithlessness. Infidelity is equated with adultery, and adultery with extramarital sexual intercourse. Unfortunately, this narrows the concept of adultery to a biological function. To focus legalistically on the sex act as the sole manifestation of adultery is to miss the point. Adultery is breaking the relationship. It means that the couple are mutually alienated and estranged, because they no longer care for one another. In words that sound like pages torn from the journals of broken marriages, Wayne Oates describes this broken covenant:

> They lose touch with each other and withdraw as selves from each other. Isolation increases and the degree of suspicion mounts in proportion to the isolation. Soon assaults are made upon each other's integrity. . . . The hallmark of this stage of conflict is repeated failure of communication. The situation progressively deteriorates until the couple simply live in silence. . . . The only vestige of a covenant that remains is a mutual feeling of hopelessness.[9]

God's Grace and Love Uniquely Available

Karl Barth has shown how people going through divorce are especially open to experiencing God's grace. Speaking of the Christian community, he says,

> When these men [and women] have had to taste to the dregs the bitter cup of divine condemnation, it will be all the more eager to point them to the gospel and the divine command, to God's promise and Yes. It will be ready to be called itself with these sinners to repentance.[10]

The simple gospel of the Christian faith is that Jesus Christ saves us from sin and death. As Paul states, "There is therefore now no condemnation for those who are in Christ Jesus" (Rom. 8:1). Unlovely as we are, broken and shattered by the guilt and despair of an unforgettable failure, God loves us. God is not limited by our regulations or even by the way in which some clergy or church folk act.

During my own agonizing days after separation, a passage from Hosea became very meaningful to me:

> How can I give you up, O Ephraim!
> How can I hand you over, O Israel!

. . . .
My heart recoils within me,
    my compassion grows warm and tender.
I will not execute my fierce anger, . . .
for I am God and not man.

(Hos. 11:8–9)

I realized that the love of God cannot be equated with the love of husband and wife in the marriage relationship. Married love is a symbol of God's love, as Paul states in Ephesians 5. But this symbol can be overloaded; identifying God's love with marital love can leave couples in despair when their own imperfect love fails. Does God's love fail too? A lot of "good" Christian people kept telling me that if I was a Christian, I should love my first wife with the same love Hosea had for Gomer and be reconciled to her. But I could not. The covenant had been broken. My love had failed. To accept that human love can break down irretrievably, however, does not mean the same is true for God's love. The Christian gospel affirms that no one can go so far in sin as to be completely beyond God's forgiveness and compassion. Even when the love of the prodigal son and the older brother for each other failed, the father's love was there for both.

The availability and wonder of God's love in my divorce experience came home to me in a rediscovery of what justification by faith meant. Because of my extremely conservative theological background, I construed divorce as a terribly evil thing. As a minister, I felt a double sense of embarrassment and shame. For some time I tried to justify myself. I tried to make it right. I convinced myself that I had been more than generous in financial settlements with my first wife; I had gone the second mile in reaching out to my two sons; and in the early days of separation, I lived a monastic life in the midst of rather meager surroundings. I even tried to "make it right" by getting my father's approval (which he never gave). I reached out to my peers, only to discover that they either shied away or gave me the impression I had "spiritual leprosy." I found a good argument for my legalistic brethren who told me the only grounds for divorce was adultery. I reminded them that if adultery is the only grounds for divorce, then I had reason to divorce, for both my wife and I had broken the marriage vows and committed spiritual adultery. None of this worked. One day while doing supervision with a spiritual advisor (himself divorced and remarried), I discovered the liberating truth that no one or nothing had to justify me. God had already done that in Jesus Christ. God's love, revealed in Christ's death and resurrection, had taken my punishment, wiped the slate clean, and given me another chance at life. Paul's statement "Therefore since we are justified by faith, we have peace with God through our Lord Jesus Christ (Rom. 5:1) was no longer just words; it became the Word. From that moment, I quit trying to "make my divorce right" and accepted God's acceptance of it and of me.

Stages of Guilt

God's love frees us from the curse of sin, and that means deliverance from guilt. Naturally, everybody feels some guilt during divorce, but as Christians we have to put up with a lot more. We have to contend not only with our own sense of failure, but also with the gnawing sense that we have offended God and the church. Lewis Rambo has identified four stages that divorcing persons experience in regard to guilt and blame:

(1) We blame the spouse.
(2) We shift the blame to ourselves,
(3) We fluctuate between a sense of our own guilt and responsibility and a belief in our spouse's having been wholly at fault;
(4) Guilt and blame balance out, and we realize that all the grey areas make labeling impossible; only then do we forgive both ourselves and our former spouse.[11]

Christians are good at rationalizations. Like the young lawyer in Jesus' parable, we are clever at justifying ourselves. Robert Capon has shown how people mismanage their divorces by minimizing their responsibility in three ways.[12] First is the "*I didn't do it*" mentality, which makes the other spouse the scapegoat. He or she is sicker, more resistant to therapy, or more stubborn than I. Second is "I didn't do *it*." Once again, the person denies responsibility by claiming that there never was a marriage in the first place, or that one of the partners morally died, or whatever. Finally comes "Yes, I did it; but at least I didn't do *that*." Here the person points with self-righteousness at other marriages which ended in divorce because of affairs or abandonment or alcoholism, and like the ancient Pharisees in the Temple, says, "My God, I thank you that I didn't divorce my wife/husband like other people did."[13] A Christian divorce, however, means acknowledging failure. God's judgment on sin means that we as Christians can reach the place where we can recognize and affirm our guilt in the failure of the marriage. Only then can God's judgment become God's grace. That grace delivers divorcing persons both from imaginary guilt, which is the most frequent kind by far, and from genuine guilt. They accept forgiveness from God, from others, and finally, even from themselves.

The Hard Work of Godly Penitence

Unfortunately, grace and forgiveness are neither cheap nor easy. Often, in an effort to be kind to divorcing Christians, people offer cheap grace in place of the gospel. They try to soften the trauma with platitudes or sugarcoat the disgrace with indifferent shrugs. One social worker, learning of my separation, told me, "So what else is new? Forget it, and move on with your life." But I couldn't forget it or move on until I had done some hard work. *People in the church often try to justify the sin, and not the sinner.* In so doing, they "have healed the wound of my people lightly" (Jer. 6:14). Henri Nouwen has well said, ". . . to forget our sins may be an even greater sin than to commit them. Why? Because what is forgotten cannot be healed and that which cannot be healed easily becomes the cause of greater evil."[14] Godly penitence involves some hard work and growth before new life emerges. Paul told the Philippians "to work out [their] own salvation with fear and trembling" (Phil. 2:12). Notice that Paul said work *out*, not work *for*. The grace of God is available, but it is realized only by those who practice the grace of self-mastery. Man and woman working out, God working in—that is the New Testament synthesis. Rosemary Ruether states clearly: "Grace and judgment, forgiveness and repentence (sic) are interdependent. But this does not mean that we are accepted on the condition of repentence (sic) as a kind of 'good work' by which we earn forgiveness."[15] The reverse is actually true. Grace is God's free gift from which Christians find the courage to face guilt. Divorcing Christians can boldly admit their guilt because they know God accepts them unconditionally. They do not need others to judge them; they judge themselves in light of God's grace. They are painfully aware that they have failed in their marriage. No glib words can reassure them to the contrary. Remembering my own divorce and watching countless people going through the same experience have made me aware that the one thing divorcing Christians do not want is some "reassuring words" that make light of failure. Justifying the sin does not justify the sinner. Such justification is as harmful to the growth of a divorced Christian as is the legalistic attitude that makes people drag the past along with them forever.

The hard work of penitence involves several things. The sins of the past are let go and left behind; reparation is made to those who have been offended. God's grace and forgiveness make it impossible for divorced Christians to remain as they were, and penitence demands that they leave their failures behind and get on with life. As Olshewsky says,

> Herein lies the flaw of both the legalist and the libertine; both deny the possibility of repentence (sic). By denying the possibility of divorce in a Christian sense . . . the legalist prohibits leaving the past behind and undertaking a new life. By ignoring the reality of divorce in a Christian sense, the libertine fails to acknowledge the need to repent of the sins of the past and to be born again.[16]

Penitence is not an easy task; it means giving up the illusion that things are other than they are, getting over the resentment against the former partner, and seeking reconciliation with him or her beyond the divorce. Christian divorce requires an acceptance of one's former mate on a new basis, as a person independent of the former marriage bond. This is complicated and difficult; it is wishful thinking to hope that both partners will be together in their repentance patterns. Repentance means that the past is let go and that there is a new beginning. More often than we acknowledge, Christians who divorce cling to the past, wallow in their guilt, and never begin a new life.

Giving up the past, whether in nostalgia or anger, means giving up feuds with former spouses, unresolved guilt about the children, and the lingering hostility that is forced upon divorcing persons by our legal adversary system. The love of God says that everyone must face the past, then let it go. Divorced Christians who cannot do that are simply out of sync with the gospel of forgiveness.

Sandra Brown has written,

> It is regrettable that forgiveness may not make for the restoration of the marriage. For whatever reason, personal fallibility in effecting the union may be such that the two persons simply cannot perpetuate the marriage, that in fact they were never able to become "one flesh". This failure to fulfill the divine intent is transcended by divine forgiveness.[17]

In time the hard work is accomplished, and a new beginning emerges.

Resurrection and New Life

Is there life after divorce? When the hard work of penitence is at an end, what then? For some Christians, remaining single may be preferable. For others, like myself, the experience of Christian divorce means remarriage. Myrna and Robert Kysar have made remarriage a symbol of Christian rebirth:

> The poignant symbols of death and resurrection are applicable here. The first marriage is dead, and with it have died the hopes and dreams of the individuals involved. But there may be a resurrection. God brings life out of the death of marriage. That life may take the form of remarriage.[18]

Remarriage is crucial to many Christians because of its symbolism of new birth. Accepting divorce and not remarriage is like accepting the cross of Jesus without the possibility of a third day. Remarriage is a third day. It is the final act of experiencing the saving love of God. James Emerson states that "In so far as remarriage is a matter of overcoming a past sin and re-establishing a relationship of oneness, the expression of the atonement with God becomes even more striking in a second marriage than in the case of a first."[19] Thus remarriage has theological implications and is a matter of salvation as well as of integrity. Remarriage is a symbol that the separation has been overcome, and that new life has begun. It opens up the prospect of a new life and a new union which, with God's blessing, may redeem the failure of the first.

One divorced/remarried church member echoed this significance of remarriage:

> All my life I had heard that if anyone was in Christ they were a new creation. But that finally became a reality for me when I remarried after my divorce. God gave me a second chance at life. It's almost as if I have lived two lives. I believe I was reborn.

The Christian church remains a symbol of reconciliation between God and people. Christ's reconciling work brought God and people back together again, and through his death he made peace. In a Christian divorce, the church needs to mediate that reconciliation. If a couple can be reconciled to each other, that is one manifestation of this reconciliation; but if that is not possible, another witness to it is Christian remarriage. Carroll A. Wise has suggested,

> The mystery of the resurrection in the New Testament has a minor parallel in the mystery experienced by some persons at the change within them when they are able to renounce that which blocks growth, and to find release for creative powers from within that they had never before experienced.[20]

In my own experience, in working with other couples who divorced and remarried, reconciliation after divorce has clearly been a "minor parallel" of the Christian doctrine of resurrection. Paul Tillich emphasizes,

> . . . resurrection means the victory of the New state of things, the New Being born out of the death of the Old. Resurrection is not an event that might happen in some remote future, but it is the power of the New Being to create life out of death, here and now, today and tomorrow.[21]

Christians who have tasted the sting of the death of marriage, but who have courageously and honestly worked through their pain to new life, attest to the fact that life begins again.

If marriage dies, Christians must accept that death and look to God for grace, mercy, and forgiveness. In anticipating remarriage, they look to Jesus' descriptions in Matthew 19 and Mark 10 of the permanence of marriage as words that *speak of the present and future*, not of the past. With God's help and grace, Christians will give the new marriage their ultimate effort, so that *this* marriage can be what God intended it to be—one flesh.

New life and resurrection may begin whether remarriage takes place or not. Each individual must choose his or her own lifestyle after divorce. Social psychologist Elizabeth Cauhapé has recently shown that after midlife divorce, a whole range of possibilities exist for people to explore. She describes eight different options, ranging from remarrying instantly to remaining single, from choosing a new mate who fits into the old circles to seeking a relationship so unconventional as to have been unthinkable beforehand.[22] Whether one remains single or remarries, divorce can result in new life: growth takes place.

Memory, Plato suggests, is the key to self-understanding. Months or even years after leaving their marriage, divorced persons may undergo a process of life review similar to that described by older people. During this process, individuals attempt to assess past behavior in order to unlock meaning for the present and the future. This review is both healthy and normal, and is a signal for growth.

There are five possibilities for growth that occur after the divorce has been placed in some perspective and new life has begun:

(1) One can learn and grow from the experience of divorce. During the bleakest moments of divorce, there are feelings of despair and hopelessness about oneself, the future, and even one's faith. Divorced Christians, however, report newfound strength in overcoming adversity and realize that their pain encouraged growth and maturity.

(2) Divorce provides the opportunity for identifying new goals and directions. Divorce is a decisive point in life that forces upon

people the need for new decisions; one cannot simply maintain business as usual while undergoing major changes in lifestyle and behavior. The process of setting new goals opens up infinite horizons.

(3) One can gain greater self-esteem and strength through facing divorce honestly. It is difficult for recently divorced persons to pass beyond a sense of failure. It is especially difficult for divorced Christians, who often have to contend with a double sense of guilt. In retrospect, though, divorced persons who have honestly confronted themselves during the process find themselves stronger for the experience.

(4) The experience of divorce is a major vehicle for learning how to die to the past and to grow. To experience divorce is to learn what it means to let go of the past and to move beyond anger and guilt. In learning this lesson, people are more equipped to deal with other experiences of death.

(5) One can gain a great sense of individuality beyond divorce. Through divorce, people are brought face to face with themselves—not in a social role such as that of parent or spouse, but as that self that goes beyond social roles. This experience of individuality forces one to analyze past behavior, interpret the present, and identify future directions.

Christian divorce means that there comes a time when the failures of the past are let go, so that a new life may begin. There is no magical length of time required for this change to take place. Nor is there anything absolute about the new beginning, since all continue to sin and fall short of the glory of God. Nevertheless, a time must come when the past is left behind and the future is begun.

Recovery of Faith

Along with reconciliation and new life, divorced people often notice a recovery of their faith. Whenever a crisis occurs, one's relationship with God is challenged. Divorce, a major crisis, provides an ideal opportunity for faith to be tested. Sandra Brown has shown how easy it is for divorcing Christians to doubt the grace of God and lose faith. She writes, "Inevitably, as the marriage fails, a pervasive sense of shame emerges not only because the divine intent is unfulfilled, but also because the expectations of so many persons have been unrealized."[23] As a divorcing Christian, I suffered similar doubts; I could not throw off a terrible sense of guilt and shame that I had offended God and that I had lost all closeness to the Holy Spirit.

Jesus' prayer for Peter in his failure speaks to divorced persons as well:

> "Simon, Simon, behold, Satan demanded to have you, that he might sift you like wheat, but I have prayed for you that your faith may not fail; and when you have turned again, strengthen your brethren."
>
> (Luke 22:31–32)

Jesus did not pray that Peter would not fail; he prayed that his *faith* would not fail. Jesus knew Peter would fail, because his weakness outweighed his boldness. However, he also knew that if Peter's *faith* did not fail, beyond that failure was the possibility of a new beginning. Through faith Peter's failure, Peter's wounds, could become the very way to strengthen the brethren. Just as Peter vowed his allegiance to be with Jesus to the end, so Christian couples have stood at the altar and vowed their commitment "till death do us part." Unfortunately, even Christians fail, and vows are broken. At this crucial time it is essential that faith not fail as well.

For a time, I thought my faith had failed. I was still angry at God for not saving my marriage or making things better right away once I finally had the courage to leave. I believed that God had called me to leave my destructive marriage; why did God not take better care of me? Why did I have to suffer loneliness, anxiety, despair, and pain? I confess that for a time I turned my back on the church and even hid from God. Now, many years later, I realize that my faith did not fail. Now I know I needed that painful, confusing time to sort out my theology and move from the "traditions of my fathers" to personal faith. I finally realized three things about God and my faith:

(1) God allowed my pain to happen, but God did not cause it. Some

theologians today tend to repudiate the idea of "God's permissive will." They assert that such a concept denies real justice in the world and deadens social responsibility. Eventually I knew that God had not willed my pain, but had permitted it. I caused my own pain, and God simply allowed it to happen. To deny that God allows pain in this way is to deny that God is God. Somehow, I knew that what God allowed was not beyond the reach of redeeming grace.

(2) God tested my faith through the delays. I never could understand why it took so long for something good to happen in my life after my divorce. I went through an eclipse of faith. When the sun is eclipsed, the light is not killed; it is merely hidden. God, who seemed so absent and aloof to my needs, was nonetheless still there—not as some "Fixit Person" to suddenly turn my shame into a success story or to produce a "new family" to replace the one I had lost, but as a steady, faithful presence. *My test of faith was being able to trust God enough to let the pain continue without any end in sight.* Perhaps this is the test of everyone's faith, amid divorce or not. During those days when life has no purpose, when the cold winter of the spirit is almost unbearable, faith *is* tested. Years later I realized all that suffering was part of God's redeeming work. Some words from Scripture outlasted my despair during the dark days of uncertainty:

> We are afflicted in every way, but not crushed; perplexed, but not driven to despair; persecuted, but not forsaken; struck down, but not destroyed.
>
> (2 Cor. 4:8–9)

(3) I could recover my faith in ministry to others. Some words of Ernest Hemingway in *A Farewell to Arms* meant a lot to me during my divorce: "The world breaks every one and afterward many are strong at the broken places."[24] I found my faith renewed as I began a ministry to other divorced persons. Henri Nouwen's concept of the "wounded healer" became a recovery of vocation for me Thomas C. Oden explains this kind of recovery when he writes,

> Repeatedly I have found, to my astonishment, that the feelings which have seemed to me most private, most personal, and there-

fore the feelings I least expect to be understood by others, when clearly expressed, resonate deeply and consistently with their own experience. This has led me to believe that what I experience in the most unique and personal way, if brought to clear expression, is precisely what others are most deeply experiencing in analogous ways.[25]

My own marital failure, my own uncertainty and loneliness, my own sense of rejection, my own eclipse of faith became wounds which were a source of healing to others. The church needs to be a community of healing for broken people. Unfortunately, that is not always so, and often it is not so for the victims of divorce. One divorced clergyman put it so well: "The church is the only army that shoots its wounded soldiers." My own experience became the means of strengthening others, and I realized how crucial support groups in the church were to divorced people.

Implications of a Christian Theology of Divorce

(1) Divorce may be an act of faith

Rather than an unforgivable sin, as the legalists contend, or guaranteed happiness, as the libertines maintain, divorce can be a responsible act of faith and conscience. Robert Sinks claims that some divorces are not acts of sin. He writes, "They are responsible decisions reached in the context of tragic and limited circumstances. Such actions are not to be repented . . . but affirmed as thoroughly justified if destructive relationships are to be escaped and the possibilities of new growth achieved."[26] One can loudly affirm Sinks' positive approach to divorce but still question whether *any* Christian divorce is ever free from the act of penance. True penance is repentance, evidenced by a new life free from the past sin.

This is not to deny, however, that Christian divorce is an act of faith. Undertaken in confidence of God's grace, it is an affirmation of Martin Luther's words to Philip Melanchthon in 1521, "Be a sinner and sin boldly, but believe and rejoice in Christ even more boldly, for he is victorious over sin, death, and the world."[27] Bonhoeffer said that Christians respond to the voice of Christ, even as Peter did, leaving his boats, or as Matthew did, leaving his tax office. The call of Christ may involve leaving a destructive marriage.

Karl Barth also viewed Christians' decision to divorce as an act of faith. He cautioned the church not to "regard them as polluted, or scandalously . . . refuse them the church's benediction in the case of a second marriage." The church "must respect the mystery of the personal relation to God in which it seems that this decision has finally been reached. It will respect the freedom of faith."[28] Hard as it is for those whose marriages are intact to accept, Christians who work through painful divorce to new life manifest genuine faith.

(2) Christian divorce can be a paradigm of the gospel

This is not to suggest that divorce is *the* way to experience the gospel, for God cannot be so limited. Nevertheless, it has proven to be *a* way for myself and other Christians to realize the gospel in personal experience. Paul wrote, "If God is for us, who is against us?" (Rom. 8:31). The gospel is not to be found in a successful marriage but in Paul's conviction that God's support is continual and invincible.

Is divorce a sin? Yes; divorce means falling short of God's intention for marriage. It means breaking God's covenant and becoming alienated and estranged from one's spouse. The good news of the Christian faith, though, is that sin *is* forgivable.

Is divorce a sin? No; divorce is not *always* wrong or unchristian. Sometimes it may be a necessary journey to wholeness.

Is remarriage adultery? Yes, in the sense that it marks a break with God's ideal intention for lifelong marriage; no, in the sense that Christian remarriages of God's people are still within the grace of God.

There is no way out of the hard work of penitence if divorce is to be redemptive. Christians, however, can repent in faith, not in despair, for "where sin increased, grace abounded all the more" (Rom. 5:20). This is the message which the church has somehow failed to make valid for divorcing Christians, that their failure and loss can become a paradigm of the Christian gospel. Divorce is thus seen neither as total liberation nor as total failure. Those who celebrate divorce as total liberation from bondage, without awareness of its pain and grief, do a disservice to any who experience this brokenness. On the other hand, those who condemn divorce as an unforgivable failure, without considering its possibilities for new life, do even greater harm to those who need the healing word.

*(3) The church needs to relate this theology of divorce
to a changed context*

A dramatic change has taken place with regard to marriage: marriage is no longer viewed as a contract but as a relationship. This fits in with the thesis proposed by Thomas S. Kuhn in *The Structure of Scientific Revolutions*.[29] Kuhn suggests that a new paradigm occurs when the adequacy of the accepted pattern is stretched to the breaking point by the phenomena which cannot be associated with it, and that the moment of breakthrough occurs when another fertile imagination conceives a new pattern and suddenly things are seen to make sense in a new and different way. Thus, any of the old hardline opposition to Christian divorce and remarriage belongs to an obsolete pattern and must be discarded. The church needs to state boldly its theology of divorce and to implement it in ministry to divorcing and divorced persons. As William Arnold suggests,

> The church is charged with the responsibility of inviting back into the home those who may feel "exiled." That seems to be done best when there is a firm and tender invitation to face one's difficulties and be made whole. Then each can minister to the other, because we all have shortcomings to be admitted and shared.[30]

Christians are to bear burdens *with* divorced persons, not *for* them. The day needs to come when divorced persons will feel no more shame or rejection than any other person in the church who has failed in business, politics, or whatever. That day has not yet come, but it is coming.

Divorce is a devastating experience. Everyone has generally recognized the terrible toll divorce takes on children, but mounting evidence shows that splitting up may be even more traumatic for the adults involved. Gerald F. Jacobson, author of *The Multiple Crises of Marital Separation and Divorce*, claims that divorce can exact a greater and longer-lasting emotional and physical toll on the former spouses than virtually any other stress, including the death of a spouse.[31] This stress can be exacerbated by the endless condemnations of legalistic religion.

A Christian divorce theology removes divorce from the ranks of demons. It takes the sting out of the death of a marriage. It gives hope beyond despair. It offers victory through defeat. And it does all this through affirming a creative balance between God's grace (forgiveness and new life) and God's truth (penitence and hard work).

In her book *Divorce: The New Freedom*, Esther Fisher includes the following prayer, which seems to express the theology of Christian divorce:

✤

PRAYER FOR THE DIVORCED

God, Master of Union and Disunion,
Teach me how I may now walk
Alone and strong.
Heal my wounds;
Let the scar tissue of Thy bounty
Cover these bruises and hurts
That I may again be a single person
Adjusted to new days.
Grant me a heart of wisdom,
Cleanse me of hostility, revenge, and rancor,
Make me know the laughter which is not giddy,
The affection which is not frightened,
Keep far from me thoughts of evil and despair.
May I realize that the past chapter of my life
Is closed and will not open again.
The anticipated theme of my life has changed,
The expected story end will not come.

Shall I moan at the turn of the plot?
Rather, remembering without anger's thrust
Recalling without repetitive pain of regret,
Teach me again to write and read
That I may convert this unexpected epilogue
Into a new preface and a new poem.
Muddled gloom over,
Tension days past,
Let bitterness of thought fade
Harshness of memory attenuate
Make me move on in love and kindness.[32]

V.
The Church Responds to Initial Pain

A Christian theology of divorce acknowledges that divorce is a failure, but not a sinful act in itself. God may not only call two persons into marriage, but may also call them apart so that divine love can be fulfilled. Undue self-concern and egoism corrupt every human community, including marriage. God is ready to forgive and initiate a new beginning for anyone upon his or her genuine penitence. The church must not fix blame, take sides, or further contribute to the prevailing adversary system, but should help both partners to realize they are equally responsible for the pain of their broken marriage. The church needs to mediate God's grace and love to both partners and to seek the reconciliation of the spouses with God and with each other, even when the marriage cannot be restored. Forgiveness sets each other free from lingering bitterness and hostility and gives opportunity for a new life beyond divorce. *Thus, the mission of the church to divorced persons is to help facilitate redemptive partings and new beginnings.* John H. Westerhoff III and William H. Willimon make it clear that "the church has a legitimate, biblically grounded, pastoral word to speak to persons whose lives are touched by the trauma of marital separation. The greatest tragedy of all would be for the church to say nothing."[1]

No one can deny the difficulty of speaking that word. From the vantage point of a recently divorced person, the task of building a new life may seem insurmountable. After all, the experience has taken an emotional and financial toll; old patterns of existence have been disrupted, and new styles of living are not yet realized. Family and friends, although wanting to help, are not always sure what to suggest. Relationships with children seem strained, for both the custodial and the absent parent. Typically, in the weeks or months after separation, individuals are uncertain where to seek help and may even resist acknowledging that help is needed.

Tim, a forty-one-year-old accountant, initially thought his separation from his wife was for the best, since the last few years of the marriage had consisted of what seemed to be continuous bickering and arguments. After a few weeks, however, Tim began to feel depressed. He found himself drinking heavily and breaking into tears whenever he thought of his daughters. He felt lonely and estranged, with nowhere to turn for help:

> I knew I needed some kind of help, but certainly not a psychiatrist. I had few friends; most of the people I knew were closer to my former wife. I couldn't talk with my family because they seemed upset about the separation. When I went to church, it was different. People treated me like I had some strange disease.

Loneliness and embarrassment always accompany separation. Friends may rally around for a while, but awkwardness and uneasiness make them drift away. Unfortunately, what most separated persons perceive as rejection or lack of concern by church members is, in fact, a failure to understand that divorce involves grief, and an inability to be present with someone who is in pain. Unlike the church's response to the death of a spouse, there are no offers of condolences, casseroles, or comfort. Church members may want to help, but they hold back simply because they don't know what to say or do.

Magnified Embarrassment

Married people, confronted with the divorce of a friend or acquaintance, sometimes feel that their own marriage is threatened, no matter how stable it has been up to that point. If it can happen to her (him), it can happen to us. Wondering about that makes them avoid separated persons. Those in shaky marriages are particularly prone to take this defensive action. The troubled couple who privately admit, "We have thought of divorce, but could never do it" sometimes view with envy the couple that actually do divorce. Occasionally members react to the divorce of others as they did to the divorce of their parents. Imprisoned by unresolved feelings, they too, shy away from separated persons. All these attitudes exist in the church, and they further alienate and ostracize separating persons.

More often than not, friends choose sides, giving their allegiance and support to only one member of the divorced couple. Friends seem to divide up like community property—his and hers. It is especially hard for divorcing church members to remain in the church when this "taking sides" prevails. Even when church members have healthy marriages, the fear remains that divorce could happen to them. People shy away from dying persons as reminders of their own mortality. The realization "This person is dying" invariably leads to "I will die," and those who are fearful withdraw. The same is true with divorcing persons. The fact of separation makes others confront their own marriages; "they are divorcing" is at times translated into the ominous prediction, "I will divorce."

Earlier I have noted how the divorce process is a progression of stages that begins when the marriage ends and continues until a new lifestyle is established. The process is like a roller coaster with alternating highs and lows and periodically a regressive pull back into the relationship to give it one more try.

Since individuals sometimes repeat stages, skip some, or have stages occur simultaneously, it is hard to generalize as to what constitutes a "normal" pattern.

From experiencing my own divorce, and from listening to many stories of divorced persons, I am convinced that there is a great difference between the early pain of separation and the latter stages when new goals and a new identity are formed. The "healthier" divorced individuals who recuperate and manage to resume productive lives seem to need approximately two years from the early pain of separation until the psychic divorce is complete. The earliest stage begins with what Paul Bohannan calls "the emotional divorce," when love and trust first disappear. Physical separation then causes more emotional distress. Sometimes the spouse least desiring the divorce may regress to the use of denial, convinced that the separation is only temporary. After the initial shock wears off, feelings of anger and betrayal ensue. Mourning the loss takes time and includes a veritable flood of emotions, ranging from guilt to depression.

What does the church do for separated persons at such a time? If Christianity exists to speak a word of compassion to those who are suffering not to "bruise a broken reed, or quench a dimly burning wick," then a broken marriage is prime time for Christians to practice their convictions. Often church members expect separating persons to continue as if nothing has happened and deny them the right to grieve. However, enlightenment can change traditional attitudes and behavior. A Christian theology of divorce, which focuses on a balance between grace and truth, can be realized in the church, the community of faith.

Rituals for Separating

When a marriage is broken by death, the church is quick to offer the surviving partner and the children support and solace. There are flowers, expressions of sympathy, hugs, many visits, and precious moments of remembering the loved one. Divorcing persons, by contrast, usually mourn alone. Funerals and other traditional rites witness to the Christian faith at the death of a person. But what about the death of a marriage? Do not separated persons need support and comfort? Most church members who divorce feel that the church neglects them and lament the fact there is no ritual to break the ice. The covenant of marriage has its ritual, but there is none for separation. Is not God present at the end of a relationship, as well as at its beginning? To acknowledge with appropriate solemnity the emotions of divorce, Robert Elliott proposes a divorce ritual combining the features of a funeral (recognition of the death of a relationship), a wedding (mutual declaration of intentions toward each other), and the confessional (guilt and forgiveness).[2]

Such a ritual is almost without precedent. Wayne Oates has shown how there are some private rituals when people separate, such as sleeping in different rooms or taking separate vacations, but there are no official or unofficial liturgies dealing with divorce.[3] Usually the only official ritual that persons experience is the solemn words of a judge in the divorce court that "the plaintiff be granted an absolute divorce from the defendant, and that the bonds of matrimony heretofore existing between them be dissolved." Often each partner goes alone to court, accompanied only by his or her attorney. Hearings are usually brisk and brief. The individuals come away empty-handed and unloved.

This is a time when the church could offer a healthier, more humane alternative. Westerhoff and Willimon have said,

> The church has been given the awesome power to loose as well as to bind. The church exists not only to bring persons together but also, on some occasions, to recognize and pray for separation among persons. . . . But we are convinced that the church should be equally bold and realistic in offering a word to fellow Christians who may go through the painful separation of divorce.[4]

In no sense does this mean that the church advocates divorce or condones it. Nor does such a ritual "bless" divorce. It simply recognizes the reality and supports those involved, for whom divorce is, for better or worse, a fact. This ritual would no more encourage divorce than funerals encourage the death of a spouse. As in the death of a spouse, however, such a ritual would affirm the church's presence at this ending of a relationship.

It is significant that in the Jewish tradition, a religious person has to have a religious divorce. In Judaism, divorce is a recognition of the "failure" of one's love and represents a potential opportunity for a second chance—if the divorcing parties examine themselves, their goals, and their values. Like the marriage contract (*ketubah*), the divorce decree (*get*) of Orthodox Judaism is primarily a legal document. In Conservative and Reformed Judaism, a *get* is likely to signify an expression of faith in the future and in one's capacity to meet the challenges of life. "It is a religious document and those who seek it find a source of strength in their faith in God."[5] It also represents bona fide written consent from the Jewish community through the rabbi.

A ritual of divorce in mainline Protestant churches would serve several purposes: (1) it would be an approved way of telling friends and members of the congregation that the marriage had ended; (2) it could provide some theological interpretation of divorce; (3) it would bring some closure and help the couple accept the finality of their separation; and (4) it would help both separating persons and members of the congregation deal unashamedly with the issue, rather than avoiding it. In pastoral care of members who separate, some things are *not* better when they are left unsaid. The church is supposedly the major support network for people in crisis. Participation in such a ritual might be one way to end the embarrassment everyone feels when separation occurs.

Already rituals are quietly beginning to emerge. However, it is difficult to identify one ritual as standard for all separating persons. In some separations, friendly relations continue to exist, while in others, hostility, guilt, and conflict make such an effort difficult, if not impossible. In such cases, only one person might agree to the ritual. This person might want and need to be affirmed by the church, even though the other person might have no desire to do so.

Phyllis Jean Sedgwick Flowers has written "A Ritual in

Which One Spouse Participates."[6] In this ritual some powerful statements are made by the minister:

> We come not to be flippant or to be in maudlin despair. We come with suspicion that divorce has as many theological ramifications as does marriage. Wherever human life is being broken or hurt there are theological responses and responsibilities.[7]

There are other rituals for separation in which both spouses participate.[8] Recently three Episcopalians, David Ulrich, Frederick Bender, and Faith Whitfield, have written a service for divorcing parents to affirm their love and responsibility for their children; it is called "A Service of Affirmation When Parents Are Separating."[9] The service reassures the children that their parents' separation was not the children's fault, and that they can be assured of both parents' continuing love and support. In this ritual, each parent in turn recites to the children,

> This separation is in no way your responsibility, but ours, your parents'. I want you to know that your presence in my life was a reason for keeping this marriage together. You brought joy when you were born. You bring joy now. Without you, I would be something less. So I am and always will be grateful to God for you. Nothing can ever erase my love for you, even though your mother (father) and I feel that we must now live separately.[10]

Alan S. Gurman and David P. Kniskern have recently questioned the validity of such rituals for separating persons, stating their "pessimism about the range of couples for whom such experiences would be applicable, i.e. personally acceptable."[11] They believe that the only people who would be willing to participate in such ceremonies and most likely to profit from them would be those with enormous ego strength and abundant social support network. Thus, people who need the support the most would probably not participate. If only one spouse were willing to participate, the church could provide him or her with such a ritual; if both persons were willing, then the ritual could become one way to offer the support and comfort of the church at a time of loneliness and grief.

Henry T. Close, a pastoral counselor and Presbyterian clergyman, has written *A Service of Divorce* which includes acknowledging the death of the marriage, creative un-marrying, and making a declaration of divorce. This ceremony parallels the structure of a marriage service, but incorporates elements of a funeral as well. Like a wedding ceremony,

> . . . it involves two people who are making commitments that involve each other. But the spirit, the mood of the service is more than that of a funeral. A marriage has died, and this death needs to be recognized. The people involved need the close support of their friends, their church, their God, so that they may get on with the task of grieving and of building a new life.[12]

As yet, the church has no official or unofficial liturgy of divorce. The following ceremony, however, suggests how the church might minister to human need through a divorce ritual. It can serve as a model from which any church might attempt to create its own liturgy of divorce.

�֍

A SERVICE OF DIVORCE[13]

Henry T. Close

Beloved friends, we are gathered here today with sadness, to bear witness to the painful side of our human existence, to the part of life that is associated with death. We bear witness today to the death of a marriage; and to the death of the dreams, the hopes, the expectations that brought this relationship into being. Somehow in the mystery of human failure these aspirations were not fulfilled. In spite of noble purposes, of good intentions, of sincere effort, this marriage has died, and the process of grieving has begun. And we here today stand with you in your grieving, to affirm our ties with you, our support for this anxious time of transition and rebuilding, and to affirm very clearly your place in the community of God's people. Marriage is a difficult venture, and there can never be guarantees of its success. It is to your credit that you tried.

You have been as two trees that were transplanted so close

together that their branches became intertwined, and their trunks grew together and became engrafted into one another. And as the rain fell on the soil, and the sun shone on their leaves and the wind blew in their branches, they would be sometimes competing and sometimes sharing; sometimes pushing against each other and sometimes supporting each other; sometimes fighting and sometimes loving. But as the trees grew, they inevitably influenced each other—permanently. And when the time came that the trees were separated, torn apart, there were painful wounds where the trunks had grown together; and roots were torn and branches were broken. And as both trees are transplanted again, they face the struggle of putting down new roots to sustain them and growing new branches with which to reach out to their world.

A Charge to the Couple

As you (man), and (woman) have committed yourselves to this separation and transplanting, you will experience a confusing array of feelings of relief and of regret, of hope and of fear, of frustration and perhaps most of all, of uncertainty. But the step has been taken, and it is important now to follow this new course and to find fulfillment in a new way of life.

As you commit yourselves to the process of creatively unmarrying, I offer to you the following tasks:

I invite you to *forgive* each other. At this point, you will have many resentments about what your spouse was and was not, or has done and not done. Perhaps you have even told yourself that if only he or she had been different, everything would have worked out beautifully. But you cannot resent without clinging to the past, and so it is important to forgive.

I invite you to forgive *yourselves*. Each of you will experience guilt for what you have been and not been, for what you have done and not done, for time and energy wasted in futile activity and inactivity. But this is now behind you, and you can forgive yourselves.

I invite you to *grieve*. There is much that has died and is still dying, and you will both experience a deep sense of loss. What you wanted to be, and what you wanted each other to be and the relationship to be are all dreams that were unfulfilled, that have died. And your task is to face these deaths, to finish the work of grieving, and to go to what lies ahead.

I invite you to *learn*. What you expected from yourselves and from each other and from marriage you did not find. Perhaps much of what you expected is not available anywhere. The ways you presented yourselves or asked for each other were not adequately effective. And it is important to learn anew what you can realistically expect from life, and how to achieve it.

I invite you to *find yourselves* again. Your identities have been closely intertwined with each other, and you have each given up some sense of yourself as individuals. To find yourselves again, you must separate from each other without the guilt or bitterness that clings to the past, and without the naive optimism that clings to an illusion.

I invite you to *love* again. There have undoubtedly been times when you have each felt very unloving and unloveable, and perhaps have despaired of ever again risking intimacy and love. But as human beings there is a hunger within you to reach out to other people, to touch and to be touched. And I charge you this day to awaken and nourish this hunger to love and to be loved.

Let Us Pray

Prayer

Loving God Our Father, Thou knowest Thy people, and Thou alone knowest the full implications of decisions painfully born in the crucible of disappointment. Bless now these Thy people as they move through this time of parting and of rebuilding. Guide them in the pathways of courage and hope and renewal. Where there has been guilt, may there be acceptance;

where there has been bitterness, may there be forgiveness; where there has been a deadness of spirit, may there be life and movement and growth; in the name of Christ, Amen.

Retaining of the Rings

In the wedding ceremony, there is an exchanging of rings, signifying a couple's intention to live together and to influence each other. This you have done. You have lived together, and in a multitude of ways, your lives have touched each other's, and you have both been changed—you have been influenced. There is now no way, even if it were desirable, for this part of your lives to disappear. There is no way for it not to have been. And so the rings, which have symbolized this portion of your existence, are not given back, they are retained. You may choose to wear them or not wear them, but they are reminders that you both gave and received. And they invite you to appreciate and cherish that which was good; and to lay aside that which was not, as now in the presence of God, you affirm your separation.

An Acceptance of Separateness

I, _____, do now solemnly and respectfully divorce you, _____. And I sever for all time, for better and for worse, the ties that have united us. I am I; you are you; and we are separate.

Prayer

Eternal God our Father, Thou art the God of life, who has created life in the beginning, and who even now brings life out of death. We pray Thee to bring new life to these Thy people. Bless the decisions that have been affirmed here in Thy presence—bless this divorce, that out of it may come wisdom. Bring to these Thy people a new sense of Thy presence, of Thy forgiveness, and of Thy Guidance. May they know anew that Thou art their God; they are Thy people.

Our Father, who art in Heaven, hallowed be Thy name. Thy Kingdom come, Thy will be done, on earth as it is in heaven. Give us this day our daily bread. And forgive us our failures, as we forgive those who contribute to our failures. And lead us not into temptation, but deliver us from evil. For Thine is the kingdom and the power and the glory, for ever. Amen.

Declaration of Divorce

As a minister of Jesus Christ, I now declare that this marriage has ended. (Man) and (woman) are no longer husband and wife. Let us therefore humbly respect the breaking of these ties.

Let Us Pray

Benediction

Now may the Lord bless you and keep you; the Lord make his face to shine upon you, and be gracious unto you; the Lord lift up the light of his countenance upon you, and give you peace; now and forever more. Amen.

Creative Ministries to the Newly Separated

Robert Weiss has shown that there are three responses by friends to people going through separation and divorce. At first, there is *rallying around*, with offers of help. People may invite their newly separated friend to dinner and even make their home available as a temporary refuge. If the separated friend wants to talk, they will usually listen. "There may be some exceptions; friends who immediately become overinvolved or rejecting or judgmental. But most friends behave well."[14]

Weiss calls the second phase *idiosyncratic reactions*, wherein the separated person is perceived as different and strange by his or her friends. At this stage some married couples are threatened, as if separation might be a contagious disease. Others react with envy and admiration, wishing they had the courage to do likewise:

Friends may imagine that the separated person is having a marvelous time or a terrible time on the basis of their fantasies of what *their* life would be like, if they were single again. Or they may decide that the separated person is sexually attractive, or needful, or self-centered, or wounded, or reprehensible, or bereft, all on the basis of their unconscious reactions to the idea of separation.[15]

During this stage, it is hard for married people to respond to the needs of the separated. Finally, *mutual withdrawal* takes place, as single-again persons and married couples begin to move in different worlds and feel uncomfortable with each other.

The church needs to relate to all of these phases with a strategy of support and help. During the rallying round phase, the church can offer pastoral care through individuals. During the stages of idiosyncratic reactions and mutual withdrawal, the church can initiate and provide divorce support groups, wherein divorced persons minister to the divorced.

To the Married

(1) Avoid Guilt Trips

Let me speak a word of grace to church members who may get berated for not responding to separated persons. Often, separating persons misperceive how church members act and are prone to imagine rejection and isolation that may not actually exist. Most of the time church members feel embarrassment and helplessness when their friends separate. Indeed, church members who have not experienced separation or divorce cannot be expected to understand. Before my own separation and divorce, I would never have had the insight that later came through experience. What happened to divorced persons seemed "closet information"; divorce was a world I knew existed, but it remained unknown, like some foreign language. My compassion and empathy for the divorced grew out of my own wounds. One of the best things a church can do for a separated person is get him or her in touch with another member who has been through the same experience. Concerned friends need not go on a guilt trip, thinking they have failed when they do not know how to respond to someone whose marriage has ended. Such "failure" is understandable. Nevertheless, there are some important ways the church as a supportive body can help. John R. Landgraf has emphasized,

> The best time to make initial contact with singles may well be when they are newly single. This is when they are most accessible. The emotional condition of the newly single person is often one of disorientation. . . . Newly single adults are often hungry for new friendships, and adventure, or help from someone who accepts them and cares.[16]

(2) Watch the Mrs. Lincoln response

Brooke B. Collison refers to the "Mrs. Lincoln response," any comment that shows an insensitivity to the needs of others. The response is, "Other than that, Mrs. Lincoln, how did you like the play?"[17] Some of these "Mrs. Lincoln responses" that church members make to the divorced are:

> "*Are you OK?*" This prompts an automatic response; the person replies "Sure, I'm OK," when he or she is obviously hurting. The reply may make the *questioner* feel better, but it conveys little of the divorced person's deeper feelings.
> "*Yes. I know exactly how you feel.*" No one can really understand what separated persons experience without having "been there," and even then every experience of divorce is different.
> "*I always knew you and Sam should have divorced.*" This is "taking sides" and playing counselor, when in fact no one has the right to make such a judgment.
> "*You shouldn't feel that way.*" Often, separated persons get this response from church members who imply that "good Christians have faith" and never get anxious or angry or guilty.
> "*A friend of mine got a divorce.*" The speaker may be trying to identify with the separated person, but what this response does is remove the focus from his or her needs. At this moment the newly separated or divorced cannot respond to other people's problems; they need help with their own.

All of these responses show the need to distract because the speaker sees separation/divorce as threatening. Contact with a divorcing person causes reflection on one's own marriage, and many people prefer to stay away from that altogether.

The best help anyone can offer at the critical time of separation is simply being with the person. What is said is not nearly as important as quiet, supportive presence. In listening and responding to confidences and sorrows, a friend should never push the divorcing person to move on through the process of divorce until that person is ready. Dietrich Bonhoeffer describes the ministry of listening and its place in the church:

> The first service that one owes to others in the fellowship consists in listening to them. Just as the love to God begins with listening to His Word, so the beginning of love for the brethren is learning to listen to them. It is God's love for us that He not only gives us His word but also lends us His ear. So it is His work that we do for our brother when we learn to listen to him. Christians . . . so often think they must always contribute something when they are in the company of others, that this is the one service they have to render. They forget that listening can be a greater service than speaking.[18]

Listening to separated persons and being present with them is a vital form of ministry to the separated.

Divorce Support Groups

As time elapses, mutual withdrawal does take place. What separated persons need is a safe place to ventilate their feelings in the presence of others who have experienced separation and divorce. People who have worked through most problems of their own divorces can be especially helpful to people in the early stages of separation. Experience has shown that one must be divorced for some time before one can acquire perspective. Although social agencies and counseling centers have already taken the lead in establishing such support, the church can also initiate groups for the divorced.[19] These groups can provide the protective context in which a person can recognize both the pain and the grace of this phase of life. In recent years, groups for separated and divorced Catholics have emerged throughout the United States.[20] They are now beginning to emerge within the Protestant church.

Matthew Fox once contrasted two symbols of spirituality, which he called Jacob's Ladder and Sarah's Circle. Jacob's Ladder is characterized by rugged individualism and ruthless independence; Sarah's Circle, on the other hand, represents interdependence and mutual support. Fox says,

> When one is climbing a ladder one's hands are occupied with one's own precarious survival and cannot readily be extended to assist others without putting one's climb and even one's life . . . into jeopardy. In contrast, when one dances a circular dance one's hands are freed to extend to others in assistance and in celebration.[21]

Divorce support groups exemplify Sarah's Circle, since the groups work from every individual's admission of powerlessness, and each member relies on other group members for strength.

A divorce support group is a microcosm of the early church. Driven underground by persecution from the Roman Empire, early Christians drew closer together to comfort, encourage, and console one another. They became one Body, the mystical Body of Christ. Church-supported divorce groups can thus help to illustrate for their members the strengthening, uplifting solidarity of Christianity.

(1) Goals

Although individual members will have their own goals, it is helpful to list significant goals for the group; reaching these objectives is critical if members are to grow through divorce, not merely go through it. The general goals for a church-support divorced group are: (1) To provide support, since divorced people experience acute loneliness and loss. As group members begin to share experiences in separation, self-disclosure leads to intimacy and understanding. Members realize they are not alone and develop a common bond. (2) To provide a place to safely discharge some of the emotions of divorce. Anger, frustration, relief, guilt, and loneliness are some of the emotions of divorce that need to be ventilated without the fear of having them boomerang in the future. (3) To deal with grief, since divorced persons need to mourn. (4) To develop new social skills. The group members learn how to handle delicate social situations (e.g., letting the family know, communicating with the former spouse) and how to help people meet new friends. Disclosing real feelings is encouraged; this promotes genuine encounters rather than the game-playing that is often reinforced by singles organizations. (5) To debrief feelings about the religious ramifications of divorce and to discover—or rediscover—religious faith. Divorce is, for Christians, a powerful religious event.

(2) Group composition

The most effective group size is between ten and fifteen members. Group members come from diverse socio-economic situations, since divorce is no respecter of persons. It is important that there be a balance of both sexes in the group. Although divorce groups are predominantly composed of women, more and more men are entering. Since many people emerge from marriage with inaccurate stereotypes of the opposite sex based on former spouses, involvement with other members of the opposite sex is crucial. Personal disclosure by both men and women allows participants to project themselves into the life of the opposite-sexed counterpart and to realize that pain, injustices, and victimization are not limited to one sex. The usual duration of a divorce group is eight weeks. Though a single session usually runs for two hours, it may be wise to begin the group with a longer meeting, preferably on a Saturday afternoon. This marathon breaks down barriers and reduces threats, and it allows the group members to experience the immediate trust that almost invariably develops in divorce groups. Part of the group process may include social experiences such as going to movies and/or to other outings, since social re-entry is a real need for divorced people. Usually group members renegotiate at the end of eight weeks, and the group may be continued as long as the majority of members feel the need of it.

(3) Format

The church-supported divorce group should include (1) an intake screening interview with the facilitator(s); (2) structured activities; and (3) unstructured time for expression by group members. Although a pre-group interview is not mandatory, it can clarify misconceptions about the group. People who are undergoing intensive psychotherapy, who indicate excessive hostility or other inappropriate behavior may need to be referred to individual counseling or therapy.

The importance of this interview was accentuated in a group I recently facilitated. A woman appeared at the first group session and began to exhibit an extreme, neurotic religious fanaticism which was obnoxious to other group members. Rather than working through her problems, she used religion as a crutch to block out the pain of her divorce. What proved harmful to other group members were her persistent attempts to persuade them that "divorce was a sin," that they should feel guilty, and that, if they were really Christian, they should try to get back together with their former spouses. Such a problem could have been avoided by a careful screening interview.

The interview is also a time for laying down the ground rules of the group. Sheila Kessler has set two criteria for membership in divorce groups, criteria which are also relevant to a church-supported divorce group: (1) that the person has definitely decided on divorce; (2) that the person is physically separated from the spouse.[22] Former spouses are not allowed in the same group, since an ex-partner's presence might prevent the other spouse from open expression of feelings and development of his or her own autonomy. During the interview, the facilitator(s) may also briefly describe the group process to reduce the anxiety that people often feel when they have not experienced a support group.

Each group session is equally divided between structured activities and unstructured time for expression by the group members. The structured sessions might include some of the material in this book (especially Chapters I–IV). The group experience must be flexible enough always to allow time for members to ventilate their current feelings.

Focus on the common stages of divorce would provide predictability and a common vocabulary and would heighten awareness that divorce *is* a process. Since many people experiencing divorce view their difficulties from a religious perspective and are looking for religious answers, the Christian theology of divorce (Chapters III and IV) would provide good content. The unstructured time in the group would be given to sharing experiences, receiving feedback from the group, and discussing interpersonal relationships. Unlike some other church groups, this group always has a need to talk and to share, and time should be given for the whole group to "check in" with each member.

(4) Issues

Since the group may include persons who are separated, who are recently divorced, and who have been divorced for some time yet remain fixated on specific divorce difficulties, the question arises about whether such diversity is good for the group. Although the recently separated may feel some initial uneasiness in the presence of someone further down the road to adjustment, experience has shown that persons undergoing all of these varying stages are important to the group dynamics. Members learn from one another how it feels to be at different stages in the divorce process; they gain perspective, learning that "now is not forever." Having varied stages of divorce represented in the group presents a problem only if the members expect that the entire group will have the same needs.

The question of who facilitates the support group for divorced persons in the church is much debated. The optimum arrangement is to have both male and female co-facilitators, because this provides both male and female role models and avoids sexual alienation and sexual stereotypes. It is also preferable that the facilitators be people who have themselves worked through divorce. The church needs to provide some kind of training for the group leaders. The groups need not be led by the minister or by professional counselors, but the leaders should receive training from someone with professional experience, preferably someone who has done pastoral counseling.

Group cohesiveness and empathy develop quickly. Since

separated and divorced people often receive polite silence or overt rejection from other people, the commonality of the divorce experience is the glue that keeps the group intact. Very early in the group process, someone invariably asks for the names and telephone numbers of other group members. With the consent of each member, every person is given a directory, and everyone comes to depend readily upon this external support system.

Termination is always an issue for divorce support groups. At the end of eight weeks, the group may decide either to disband or to contract for more time together. Sooner or later the members should be integrated into the life of the church; in no sense should the group be isolated. A divorcing Christian needs the worship and fellowship of the church community. Paul W. Pruyser points out that the church has a unique language of faith to offer its people. He claims that many people are looking for solutions for their problems which lend themselves to Christian interpretation. The church should not be afraid of using its language of faith, words such as repentance, guilt, grace, and resurrection.[23] Few people are more open to the gospel than those experiencing divorce. Defenses are shattered, life is broken, and healing is desperately needed. That reality came home to me with full force one Lord's Day when my congregation was singing the words of Thomas Moore's hymn, and I noticed some of the members of the divorce group sitting together. As they sang

> Come, ye disconsolate, where'er ye languish,
> Come to the mercy seat, fervently kneel;
> Here bring your wounded hearts, here tell your anguish:
> Earth has no sorrows that heaven cannot heal.[24]

I was joyfully aware of the church as Christ's living body of compassion for all broken children.

Divorce support groups may be the best gift the church can offer divorcing people at the point of their initial pain. A divorce group, as a microcosm of the true church, becomes a reconciling and caring community. One forty-year-old woman affirmed,

For the first time in my life I experienced grace. All my life I had heard sermons, gone to church, and been "a good Christian." But in that group I was loved and accepted despite my failure. My husband made me feel so worthless, but the group rebuilt my confidence. I tell my divorced friends that a divorce group at the church was the answer for me.

"The tragedy of Christian ministry," writes Henri Nouwen, "is that many who are in great need, many who seek an attentive ear, a word of support, a forgiving embrace, a firm hand, a tender smile, or even a stuttering confession of inability to do more, often find their ministers distant men [and women] who do not want to burn their fingers."[25] Providing support and care for separated/divorced persons early in their pain through new rituals, personal concern, and support groups can reverse this experience.

VI.
The Church Responds
to Life After Divorce*

Recently I thought about two people in my parish. One was a fifty-year-old divorcée who told me she was leaving the church. "It's nothing anyone did," she told me. "I just don't fit here anymore. I'm moving on." The church had ministered to her needs when she was separated, but gradually she was forgotten in all the family-centered activities, and she felt alienated. The other was a forty-five-year-old man who had remarried and had become the instant stepfather of teenage daughters. The reconstituted family attended the church, but

*Some of the material in this chapter is reprinted from the author's article, "A Ritual of Remarriage" in the December 1983 issue of *The Journal of Pastoral Care* with the permission of the Association for Clinical Pastoral Education, Inc. who hold the copyright.

no one seemed to understand the unique problems they faced.

Both of these situations reflect the church's lack of ministry to people after divorce. Whether these people leave the church or remain, they are strangers who speak a language no one understands. Wayne Oates, commenting on the divorced people in the church, says,

> . . . they are like men [and women] without a country or lost sheep of the house of Israel as far as their relationship to the churches is concerned. The majority of divorced people find new meaning in remarriage. This has become the prevailing pattern in our society. But it puts them in opposition to the church, whose teachings hitherto allowed these people no room.[1]

In its focus on remarriage, this chapter neglects two groups of divorced persons: those who remain fixated in their anger, self-pity, and despair, and those who do not remarry. The former need counseling and therapy beyond what the church can offer; the latter have become the subject of many excellent books dealing with a ministry to single people. Because of the prevalence of second marriages, the major concern of this chapter is how the church has responded to the divorced person who remarries.

Statistics indicate that 85% of divorced persons remarry, half of them within one year after the divorce. Thus the divorce is actually the transition between marriages. Currently, remarriages represent 32% of all marriages in the United States; and as the divorce rate continues to rise, the remarriage rate will also increase.[2] Andrew Cherlin says that "most divorced adults will spend most of the rest of their lives not living alone or in a single-parent family but in a family of remarriage."[3] Nevertheless, the sobering fact remains that 44% of all remarriages end in divorce. This high rate of failure may indicate that society and the church have not designed helpful ways to assist remarrieds in dealing with the complex issues of the new family. Popular sentiment to the contrary, love is not always better the second time around.

Remarriage, furthermore, is an integral part of the Christian theology of divorce. It is the resurrection experience for divorced people, the opportunity for a new life beyond the dead past. In the religious passage of divorce, persons are stripped of public success at marriage. They die to an important part of life. But even in the darkness of this moment, they can be invited to confess their responsibility without debilitating guilt; they can be made aware of God's healing grace; and in this Christian dynamic of growth, they can die and begin to live again. Although healing may take place without remarriage, second marriages can bring true healing. Thus, forgiveness and restoration of divorced persons in the church include the right to remarry. Remarriage should be blessed by the church in light of penitence and forgiveness.[4]

Unfortunately, the church has not always demonstrated this grace in its attitudes toward the remarriage of divorced persons. Whether by overt rejection or uneasy silence, the church has not recognized, let alone affirmed, these "strangers" in its midst. The issue of remarriage is crucial, because how the church responds to this clearly reveals how well it practices the Christian theology of divorce.

The Remarriage Issue

How do churches and clergy respond to the growing number of members who remarry? A strange ambiguity remains, as Stanley A. Ellisen had said:

> Ironically, there are few issues on which the church is so confused and uncertain as on the problem of divorce and remarriage. Small wonder, since so many pastors also share that confusion. Some pastors will marry divorced people; some will marry some, but not others; and yet others will not pronounce a pastoral blessing on any second-go-round of marriage apart from the death of one of the partners.[5]

Wayne Oates has shown how the churches and their pastors have taken four major approaches to the remarriage of divorced persons. Ministers who marry any and all persons for a fee, or who will have nothing to do with divorced persons and refuse to remarry them, exemplify the *Laissez-Faire* approach. The *Idealists* allow no place for divorced persons' remarriage by the church, since the ideal of permanent marriage must be preserved; some, however, advocate a "service of blessing" for a couple remarried by the state. The *Forensic* approach rests upon the premise that the teachings of Jesus refer to Christian marriage, and not to marriage in general. The Roman Catholic Church, with its casuistic efforts to determine the validity or nullity of previous marriages, is a good example of this approach. Catholics today can obtain marriage annulments for broad reasons such as "lack of due discretion," "incapacity to marry," and "antisocial or immature personality." The American Catholic Church's liberalized guidelines have so concerned the Vatican that the new Code of Church Law, which went into effect in 1983, makes the annulment procedure more difficult and time-consuming. But it hasn't changed the law substantively.

Before 1965, a divorced Catholic was a pariah. Today, more than 1,000 Catholic groups for divorced and separated members exist in the United States, and two-thirds of the American dioceses have official programs designed for these people. In 1968 Monsignor Stephen Kelleher called for an end to the Marriage Tribunal and annulments and acknowledged the right of Roman Catholics to remarry in the church.

Oates' *Confrontational/Therapeutic* approach confronts the couple with the claims of the Christian gospel and demands that each one own personal responsibility for the failure of his or her first marriage. It also attempts to establish a responsible trust between the church and the remarrying couple. The church does not merely lay hands of blessing upon the marriage but also seeks to continue its ministry to the couple through a covenant with the church.[6]

In my own remarriage and in working with many couples preparing for remarriage in the church, I have found the following responses by clergy and congregations when divorced people seek the blessing of the church.

The Permissive Response

No questions are asked, no demands made, and both congregation and clergy accept the remarriage as if it were a first marriage. This is cheap grace acceptance which simply does not deal with the issue of remarriage; it can magnify the feelings of alienation and isolation which remarrieds already feel.

The Legalistic Response

The answer is always "no" and is usually justified on tightly interpreted "biblical grounds."[7] While it is true that such a position is easier, since it is clear-cut and predetermined, and that it may win grudging respect from those whose remarriage is refused, it is hardly consistent with the teachings or spirit of Jesus. Usually, couples who are turned down by ministers feel rejection, which further alienates them from the church. One corollary to this absolute refusal to remarry divorced persons is the policy of remarrying the "innocent" party in a divorce where there has been desertion or adultery. This policy presents insoluble problems. It is simplistic and unrealistic, if not even unchristian. William Oglesby has said,

> . . . the simplistic identification of one person as "guilty" and the other as "innocent" begged the obvious point of mutual involvement in broken relationships. . . . From a theological point of view the idea of "innocence" could not be substantiated in light of the fact that "all have sinned and fall short of the glory of God" (Rom. 3:23).[8]

Both partners need to seek forgiveness when a marriage breaks or is terminated. The divorce itself may have been too easily sought or too long delayed. It could have been a means for someone to escape working on problems or to avoid expending effort to save the marriage. On the other hand, a person who felt guilty may have tolerated a destructive relationship so long that he or she caused real damage to all in the family. In any case, both partners share the responsibility for the broken marriage. Thus the church should make no effort to determine the "guilty" or "innocent" party as a basis for remarriage. Indeed, in the Christian perspective, there is no distinction.

The Double Standard

Some ministers will remarry divorced persons if they are convinced that the first marriages were not Christian ones, but they will refuse remarriage to those who were Christians when they married the first time. Such a double standard allows to those who did break the marriage covenant no room either for genuine penitence or for God's grace. Consequently it denies the gospel.

Gordon Wenham advocates another "double standard" attitude toward the divorced and remarried. Although he refuses to remarry divorced persons, he does not think they should be barred from the church:

> It seems to me that our Lord did not want his disciples to remarry after divorce. . . . By declining to marry [divorced persons] in church, we express our faithfulness to Christ's ideals: by allowing those who remarry elsewhere to continue in full church membership, we declare his compassion and forgiveness.[9]

Whatever the rhetoric, such an approach makes divorced/remarried Christians "second class citizens" in the church.

I believe that none of these responses represents a Christian attitude to the remarriage of divorced Christians. As an alternative, I offer a *Pastoral* response based on a Christian theology of divorce.

The Pastoral Response

In this response, remarriage is neither lightly sanctioned nor flatly denied. Refusing to marry any and all divorced persons is a legalistic, easy way out of the dilemma; furthermore, it denies human need and the opportunity for God's grace. On the other hand, indiscriminate remarriage on demand is a permissive sanction of human failure that portrays a God of cheap grace who is blind to sin, and it prevents the godly penitence that leads to new life. David Atkinson has described a more humane, pastoral approach:

> The only feasible criteria on which the Church can decide whether or not it is appropriate to give its blessing concern not degrees of guilt, but present attitude. . . . and the condition . . . on which the Church's blessing on second marriage should be decided, is penitence for past sin and a genuine desire to seek God's grace for a new marriage which accords with his pattern.[10]

If such evidence is present, then the church should bless remarriages in the sole light of repentance and forgiveness. This approach is valid only for Christians who give evidence of their penitence and claim the promise of the gospel for forgiveness and new beginnings. In the view of the church, what is most important is whether the person or persons have learned and been released from their past. If they have recanted their past failures and accepted forgiveness, they are free to enter a new marriage with the blessing of the church.

What the church needs to realize is that for Christians, the experience of divorce and remarriage can be a dynamic religious event. Persons often encounter God most powerfully in times of crisis, when they are stripped of some part of themselves. Divorce and remarriage can be such an opportunity. Divorcing persons die both to their marriage and to their sense of worth and identity, but in so doing they find new beginnings. When divorce occurs, reconciliation with oneself can take place.

Perhaps the greatest disservice of the church's more conventional attitude regarding divorce and remarriage has been its neglect of this spiritual potential. Seeming to suggest that God could not possibly be at work in such a traumatic event, the church's official ministry has forced many Christians to face these issues alone. By denying the possibility of new life beyond divorce, the church has given divorce the appearance of an unforgivable sin. Divorce, it has seemed to say, is a spiritual dead end: it leads nowhere and could not be a part of a Christian's spiritual experience. The pastoral approach to remarriage suggests a better way.

A MODEL FOR MINISTRY TO REMARRIEDS

The following model is suggested for churches and clergy as a ministry to divorced persons who seek remarriage in the church.

(1) The pastoral interview. The couple meet with the minister, who seeks evidence that they each understand the Christian theology of divorce, give evidence of having worked through their problems, and are aware of God's grace for new beginnings. Unless there have been time and space for the couple to work through their respective divorces, the remarriage can become another failure. Often, some of the hard work a divorced person has to do before being ready for remarriage is the task of individuation, or the relinquishing of the dependent-child state. Dorothy Cantor contends that many people who did not complete the psychological task of individuation in young adulthood try to accomplish this task later, and that divorce can be an indirect result of such an attempt.[11] The minister needs to be sure that both divorced persons have completed this task and can now enter remarriage without trying to resolve their own identity crises.

(2) Conferences with sponsoring couple. When the minister is convinced that the couple are ready for remarriage, they are assigned to a sponsoring couple (themselves remarried) who meet with the couple for several sessions, discussing the problems of remarriage. One of the most common fallacies held by clergy and never-divorced people about remarriage is that it is the same as first-time marriage. The new family cannot fit into a biological family mold. The second time *is* different. Couples who have been working through a remarriage can provide help for those about to enter one.

(3) The remarital interview. When the preliminary work has been accomplished, the couple once more meet with the minister to plan the remarriage. George W. Knight's *The Second Marriage Guidebook*[12] contains helpful suggestions. The trend today

is for couples who remarry to have a more elaborate ceremony than in the former days, when couples were remarried simply and quietly by a justice of the peace. Knight understands the differences between first and second marriages, and he gives practical advice. He suggests three remarriage ceremonies,[13] some of which maintain the traditional vows with a contemporary flair. However, it is my belief that the ritual of remarriage should reflect the Christian theology of divorce.

(4) *The ritual of remarriage.* It is all too obvious that neither the marriage service as it now stands, nor the service of blessing following a civil marriage, gives adequate expression to the event of Christian remarriage, with its essential components of confession, penitence, thanksgiving, and new beginnings. Divorce and remarriage, as stated earlier, reflect the death and resurrection of Jesus. Divorced persons know what the dying is, but they need the church to help them find the resurrection. *Just as the church should ritualize divorce in order to give closure, it should also ritualize remarriage in order to give hope.*

Such a ritual should strike a healthy balance between truth and grace, for it witnesses to both the pastoral and prophetic roles of the church. By affirming that God intends both permanence in marriage and penitence for divorce, the church can maintain important distinctions between first and second marriages.

(5) *Assimilation into the church family.* Although the members of the church may find it awkward and difficult to reach out to the remarried, caring for them is a vital part of the ministry of the church. At stake is the very nature of the church as the family of God which includes everyone, regardless of marital status. The increasing number of remarriages in the church makes this a matter of unprecedented urgency.

Pastoral Remarital Counseling

The redivorce rate of 44% is sufficient evidence that many couples seeking remarriage are not ready for a new relationship. Remarital counseling of divorced persons should be a major concern for ministers, because far too many divorced persons rush headlong into new marriages and repeat their failures.

Some remarrying couples, for example, become highly defensive about problems, and as Laura Singer suggests, their premarriage behavior often contains denial.[14] Denying that problems may exist is not intentional dishonesty by either person; rather, it is a way of dealing with fear of further rejection.

Although the current trend is to question the value of premarital counseling, remarital counseling *is* essential. It is particularly necessary when remarriage takes place earlier than two years after divorce. In fact, Bruce Fisher has claimed that "on the average it takes about a year to get . . . past the really painful, negative stages. . . . Some research suggests that a few . . . will need as long as three to five years."[15] Any discussion of sensitive issues or potential problems is scary, but these matters need to be faced in the pastoral interview. Only then can the couples desiring remarriage avoid what Reinhold Niebuhr called "the pharisaic fallacy," the assumption that mere knowledge of past sins prevents their repetition.

Richard P. Olson and Carole Della Pia-Terry have pointed out two misconceptions counselors have about readiness for remarriage.[16] One fallacy is that people give evidence of recovery from divorce by making the decision to remarry. This is not always the case, since other factors (loneliness, financial security, the children) may be in the picture. Although one could not indiscriminately agree with the cliché that "the first partner to remarry after a divorce is the most insecure," there is some truth in that statement. The second misconception is that if the couple have been living together, they have sufficient knowledge about what remarriage will be like. As Olson and Pia-Terry emphasize, "Living together by no means guarantees that the couple has developed an open, honest life-style on which an enduring commitment can be made."[17]

The pastoral remarital interview should examine two major issues: the successful resolution of the former marriage, and the relationship between the two people remarrying. Consideration of these matters will help the pastor assess whether there has been a letting go of past sin in penitence and a seeking of new life in faith. Among the questions he or she can ask are the following:

What caused the most pain for you in your former marriage?

What will keep you closely attached to your first marriage, and what will make it easy for you to leave it?

Have you really forgiven your former spouse for the pain and humiliation you suffered?

Have you forgiven yourself for the hurt you caused him/her?

Can you recall the good memories of your former marriage without being immobilized by anxiety, resentment, or grief?

By listening closely to the couple's responses to these questions, the minister can determine whether both persons have accepted the death of their former marriage relationships and have done genuine work in resolving some of the issues of their divorce. Horton says,

If he [or she] only finds that the other partner is blamed, the divorce is glossed over as "just one of those things" and there is blind optimism that, of course, all will be well next time, he [or she] will hesitate to countenance re-marriage in church.[18]

The pastor can then raise questions about the current relationship:

Can you say a little about how you met?

What are some of the strengths of your relationship?

Do you see any similarities between your partner and your former spouse?

Can you level with each other on all issues?

How do you handle conflict and anger?

Have you discussed any questions related to finances and the children and reached agreement?

Do you see any relationship between your remarriage and the Christian faith?

After the interview, the minister can contact a remarried couple in the parish to become the sponsor couple for a series of sessions on remarriage.

A Couples-sponsored Peer Ministry

Judith Tate O'Brien and Gene O'Brien have written a handbook for couples planning remarriage in the Roman Catholic Church.[19] It presents a workable model of couple-to-couple peer ministry in which remarried couples in the parish sponsor engaged couples who seek remarriage in the church. The major issues of remarriage and the reconstituted family are dealt with in an honest manner, and the engaged couple benefits from the experience of those already living in a remarriage. The minister can meet with the sponsoring couple to discuss the format of the sessions. Either the O'Briens' book, *A Redeeming State*, or a recent book by Olson and Pia-Terry, *Ministry with Remarried Persons*, could provide the structure for the sessions. The latter book describes a six-session group and focuses on such topics as building a remarriage relationship, building a remarriage-family structure, remarriage and children, remarriage and finances, anger and conflict in remarriage, and remarriage and religion.[20] There will always be tensions within remarriages, such as financial troubles caused by alimony payments or child support, the inclusion of stepchildren, and contact with former spouses. Nevertheless, a couples-sponsored ministry to remarrieds could provide a realistic way of dealing with some problems and perhaps preventing others.

Planning the Remarriage

Every effort should be made to make remarriage an act of worship in the church, with members of the Christian community present. An early study by August B. Hollingshead examined a number of behavioral traits associated with weddings and compared these traits to previous marital patterns.[21] Hollingshead discovered that in second marriages the weddings are likely to be less formal, to be held in a setting other than a church, and to have fewer guests and fewer persons in the wedding party. It appears Hollingshead's conclusions are still valid. Remarriages often lack the credibility of first marriages; private rituals can seem empty, and they contain less of the high joy and praise that characterize first marriages. Silence, embarrassment, and private ceremonies are not appropriate responses for the Christian church when couples seek to create new marriages out of the death of old ties. What makes anyone think that the spirit of the same Christ who was present at a wedding in Cana of Galilee would not be present at a Christian remarriage? The attendance of a caring and accepting community is an essential part of the ceremony when Christians seek to establish new relationships within the grace of God.

At present, there is no ritual which gives adequate expression to Christian remarriage.[22] Wedding ceremonies are designed for first marriages and have nothing to do with the issues of remarriage. Because of the awkwardness or embarrassment involved in the loss of partners by divorce, remarriages have usually been treated as private affairs witnessed only by the family and a few friends. Such private ceremonies negate the presence and support of the Christian community at a time when that is needed. They do not give members of the church an opportunity to "restore . . . in a spirit of gentleness" those who have been "overtaken in any trespass" (Gal. 6:1). When a couple who are avowedly Christian have gone through serious preparation for their remarriage and seek the blessing of the church, the church needs to be present with its message of resurrection and hope, even as it was present at the first marriage.

It is important that there be a remarriage ritual based on a Christian theology, which strikes a healthy balance between grace and truth. An integral part of the ceremony should be individual and corporate confession of sin. First, the couple need to confess their failure in the primal marriages, failure which includes the sin of clinging to the past, either as a form of nostalgia for what might have been or as the illusion that things are other than what they are. This confession also includes resentment against former mates, regret that the church did not respond, and guilt over failure. The couple may also confess their own previously broken vows and neglect of their families. Next, the church needs to confess its failures in the broken marriage, its neglect of the couple, its lack of support in their conflicts.

Another important part of this ritual should be the inclusion in the ceremony of children from the previous marriages. A workable name to define the new family created by the remarriage has not yet been found. Selina Sue Prosen and Jay H. Farmer lament this lack of an appropriate term:

> A "blended" family has the connotation of putting intact obstacles in a blender to make mush. "Reconstituted" conjures up thoughts of orange juice. "Merged" sounds like a corporate deal.[23]

Regardless of terminology, a new family does come into being at a remarriage, and the ceremony should include parts for both the parents and the children. Children have ambivalent feelings when parents remarry. Sometimes children urge remarriage in an attempt to restore the security undercut by divorce. Other times they resist remarriage, feeling nostalgic for their former family or creating fantasies that their parents will be reconciled. Occasionally, too, children resist remarriage because they do not want to surrender their power of position in the single-parent family at the time of the remarriage. If children are included in the ceremony, they are more likely to acknowledge the reality of the new family.

Children of twice-married parents often feel scattered or caught halfway between two worlds. At best, they are a little unsure about their place in this new family. Robert Capon, in his excellent book *A Second Day: Reflections on Remarriage*, declares that the effect of remarriage on children is such a vexed and varied subject that there is no general rule to follow except "Offer all your children, step or otherwise, friendship—and let it go at that."[24] Olson and Pia-Terry, however, suggest a three-stage process between the remarrying couple and their children. First, the couple announce their wedding plans to the children;

then they allow enough time between the announcement and the wedding for the children to absorb this news and ask questions about how the remarriage will affect their lives. Finally, in discussion with the children, the couple plan ways for them to be involved in the wedding.[25]

Although some couples may wish to write their own remarriage ceremonies, I suggest the following ritual of remarriage, a ceremony I wrote after officiating at a number of remarriages over the past five years.[26] It includes the integral parts of a Christian theology of remarriage, the support and presence of the community of faith, and the involvement of children in the ceremony.

RITUAL OF REMARRIAGE

(To be used when one or both parties have been divorced)

During the Following:

    "A" Indicates words spoken by the minister.

    "B" Indicates words spoken by the couple, or the congregation, or the children (if involved).

A. Dearly beloved, we are here in the presence of God so that _____ and _____ may be united in holy marriage. Jesus sanctified marriage by his presence at the wedding in Cana of Galilee, and taught that a man shall leave his father and mother, and cleave unto his wife; and the two shall become one flesh. The Apostle Paul described marriage as a great mystery, and viewed it as a symbol of the relationship between Christ and the church.

(To Couple): On this day of your marriage, you stand somewhat apart from all other human beings. Your first marriage failed or

ended with death, and with it died all your hopes and dreams for that union. You have let that relationship go, that this new marriage may be. Remember, as Christians you must believe that it is God who has brought you together and given you another chance to build a future. Remarriage is a symbol of resurrection and rebirth. As God brought Jesus Christ from the grave, so God can bring new life out of the death of your former marriage. And it is that blessed hope and promise we celebrate on this day as you take this step in faith.

Confession of Sin

The Christian faith affirms that all who receive God's forgiveness must first acknowledge their guilt, confess their sin, and claim divine grace. You must now confess your failure in that first marriage, express your willingness to die to those ancient vows, and claim God's healing and forgiveness for this new relationship. Do you both confess your failure, and rest upon God alone for forgiveness?

B. We do.

A. *(To congregation present):* Even in times of great joy like the celebration of this marriage, we are reminded of how often we have failed to be loving; witnessing the creation of this new family, we are mindful of how often we have taken our own families for granted and failed them in many ways. As we witness this couple about to pledge their vows to each other, we recall how our lives are strewn with pledges seriously made and lightly broken. We have also often failed to minister to those divorcing by our silence or lack of support. Will you now confess your own failures of love, your pride, and betrayal of divine grace in the silence of this moment. *(Silence)*

Declaration of Forgiveness

Hear the gracious words of the gospel:

> Who is in a position to condemn? Only Christ, and Christ died for us, Christ rose for us, Christ reigns in power for us, Christ prays for us! (Rom. 8:34, Phillips)

Whenever our hearts condemn us . . . God is greater than our hearts, and knows everything. (1 John 3:20, rsv—*Inclusive Language Lectionary*)

If any one is in Christ, there is a new creation; the old has passed away, behold, the new has come. (2 Cor. 5:17, rsv—*Inclusive Language Lectionary*)

Affirmation by the Christian Community

A. Let the Christian community now affirm its love and good will for this couple in the spirit of the words of the Apostle Paul,

Brethren, if [a person] is overtaken in any trespass, you who are spiritual should restore him [her] in a spirit of gentleness. Look to yourself, lest you too be tempted. Bear one another's burdens, and so fulfil the law of Christ. (Gal. 6: 1–2)

B. *(Congregation)* We do receive, affirm, and bless this couple, resolving to bear their burdens, to stand by them in the days ahead, and to promise our love and support in the Christian community.

A. I now declare that this couple have expressed before God a genuine penitence for the failure of their past marital relationship, have honestly surrendered the former ties, and have received the redeeming grace of God. They now ask for renewal and dedication to a new covenant relationship which they now resolve by faith to establish with each other. In any marriage, the most important act is the commitment by both persons to a relationship of trust and love. As you repeat these vows, you pledge your souls to each other, and to a relationship which can overcome all obstacles, transcend all problems, and witness to the triumph of experience over hope.

(The following vows may be said, or the couple may prefer to write their own vows.)

A. Repeat after me, first the man, then the woman.
I, _____ take you, _____ to be my wedded wife, and bind my life to you. Believing in God's constant love, which alone makes marriage a covenant bond, I pledge to be your faithful husband, in sickness and health, in joy, and sorrow, in hard-

ships and ease, in conflict and closeness, from this day forward.

I, ＿＿＿＿＿＿ take you, ＿＿＿＿＿＿ to be my wedded husband, and bind my life to you. Believing in God's constant love which alone makes marriage a covenant bond, I pledge to be your faithful wife in sickness and health, in joy and sorrow, in hardships and ease, in conflict and closeness, from this day forward.

A. May these two people fulfill this covenant which they have made. Having grown to trust themselves and each other, may they not be afraid to trust and welcome life. May their remarriage be a symbol of a new life which begins this day beyond the pain of their past. What greater thing is there for two human souls than to feel that they are joined to strengthen each other and to be one with each other in silent unspeakable memories?

A. Hear now the words of Paul about the greatest thing in the world, love.

> If I speak in the tongues of men and of angels, but have not love, I am a noisy gong or a clanging cymbal. And if I have prophetic powers, and understand all mysteries and all knowledge, and if I have all faith, so as to remove mountains, but have not love, I am nothing. If I give away all I have, and if I deliver my body to be burned, but have not love, I gain nothing.
>
> Love is patient and kind; love is not jealous or boastful; it is not arrogant or rude. Love does not insist on its own way; it is not irritable or resentful; it does not rejoice at wrong, but rejoices in the right. Love bears all things, believes all things, hopes all things, endures all things.
>
> Love never ends. (1 Cor. 13: 1–8)

A. The ring is a visible symbol of invisible love: this love, like a ring, should never end. As the Father gave a ring to the lost son who returned from the far country, so this ring which you give to each other is a symbol of the acceptance and restoration which your remarriage signifies.

(The minister shall then give the ring to the man to put upon the third finger of the woman's left hand. The man, holding the ring there, shall say after the minister:)

B. This ring I give you, in token and pledge of our constant faith, our marital rebirth, and our unending love.

(Then, if there is a second ring, the minister shall give it to the woman to put upon the third finger of the man's left hand; and the woman, holding the ring there, shall say after the minister:)

B. This ring I give you, in token and pledge of our constant faith, our marital rebirth, and our unending love.

Affirmation of Children and Parents

A. As you begin a new life together, you are more than husband and wife. Your children of a previous marriage are of God, and are to be wholly nurtured as if they were your own. Repeat this commitment to them.

B. We each acknowledge that we will be good parents and friends to the children of this new family. As God adopted us as children by grace, so we adopt these children in our family, and promise to nourish, support, and love them. No greater gift can we give them than to nurture them in the love of God and to be their friends.

A. *(To the children):* You may have strange feelings about this new marriage. You may feel unsure about your place in this new family, or wonder how you will relate to your new parent. As you grow older you will come to realize your parent's need to find a new life with another person beyond the pain they experienced. You will discover how God can create a new family where all are accepted and loved. Repeat after me.

B. We accept _____ as our new parent, and we accept our role in the new family. We will do our best to make this new family one in which all feel loved and accepted, and in which no one will feel like a stranger.

Pronouncement

A. By the authority given to me as minister of the church of Jesus Christ, I now declare that _____ and _____ are remarried. What God has joined together, let no man put asunder.

Be ready bravely . . .
To find new light that old ties cannot give.
In all beginnings dwells a magic force
For guarding us and helping us to live.[27]

When He created man, God gave him a secret—and that secret
was not how to begin, but how to begin again. . . . it is not given
to man to begin; that privilege is God's alone. But it is given to
man to begin again—and he does so every time he chooses to defy
death and side with the living.[28]

Set me as a seal upon your heart,
    as a seal upon your arm;
for love is as strong as death, . . .
Many waters cannot quench love,
    neither can floods drown it.
If a man offered for love
    all the wealth of his house,
    it would be utterly scorned.
    (Song of Sol. 8:6,7)

Prayer

Eternal God, without your grace no marriage is possible.
Strengthen _____ and _____ with the gift of
your spirit, so they may fulfill the vows they have taken. Keep
them faithful to each other and to you. Fill them with such love
and joy that they may build a home where no one is a stranger,
and where all things become new. May they so live together as
heirs of the grace of life, that they may be a witness to the power
of love over pain and resurrection over death. Through Jesus
Christ.

Benediction

Now may the God of peace who brought again from the dead
our Lord Jesus Christ, the great shepherd of the sheep by the
blood of the everlasting covenant, bring your marriage from the
death of old ties to a new life together; may the Lord bless you
and keep you; may the Lord make his face to shine upon you
and be gracious unto you; may the Lord lift up the light of his
countenance upon you and give you his peace. Amen.

Pastoral Care After the Remarriage

Pastoral care of the remarried must not end with the marriage ceremony. There are unique challenges for the remarried family which the church needs to address. Of course, the church's acceptance of remarrieds often depends on certain contingencies. When a new family come to the church and in time reveal that they are a remarried family, or when a couple, both of whom are divorced, start coming to church and then are remarried in the church, there is little difficulty. It is somewhat different when a couple within the church undergoes divorce, and in time one of them meets someone from outside the church and requests remarriage within the church. Some church members still find the divorce of church members hard to accept and often view remarriage with suspicion. Pastoral care of the remarried family will be discussed more fully in Chapter VIII. In brief, however, the church has the following responsibilities to remarrying couples:

(1) The minister needs to contract with the couple to meet six months after the wedding to discuss the issues they have faced in their remarriage.

(2) The minister must be consistent about a policy regarding remarriage. Ministers need to face these issues with the decision-making board of the church and set a policy of remarriage. It is all too obvious that even when the minister helps couples experience forgiveness and new life through remarriage, the couple can still experience "second class church membership" when members remain aloof and uninterested.

(3) Church members need to express support by attending the wedding. Often church members shy away from remarriages if the former spouse was or is a member of the church. Instead of debating whether attending the wedding expresses disloyalty to the former spouse, church members need to stand by the remarriage.

(4) The church should offer support groups and should encourage the couple's acquaintance and fellowship with other remarried couples in the church.

Leslie Aldridge Westoff has well said that "Our remarried

people of today are, I believe, the pioneers who have had to break new ground, largely unaided, without traditions and signposts to guide them."[29] By reaffirming Christian remarriages, the church can break new ground. If the second marriage brings healing, the church has no choice but to accept it as good. As its Master said, "'Is it lawful on the sabbath to do good or to do harm, to save life or to destroy it?'" (Luke 6:9). To deny healing in the name of rigid adherence to a narrow legalism comes perilously close to the pharisaic position which Jesus opposed so strongly.

The church exists to make new beginnings possible. According to Myron Madden, "Modern man finds himself in need of resources that will bestow wholeness and oneness. Meaningful religion speaks of rebirth and brings man to a state of blessing. In order to come to blessing man needs to be freed from the feeling of curse."[30] The church needs to cease pronouncing curses on divorced persons who seek remarriage. Rather, it needs to heed the words Peter heard: "'What God has cleansed, you must not call common'" (Acts 10:15). When confession and penitence for first failures are evident, and when hope and faith for the new relationship are present, then the church needs to bless those of its own who seek new life after divorce.

VII.
What Can Be Expected of Clergy When Divorce Occurs

Susan was a forty-four-year-old nurse, an active teacher in the church school, and the mother of two children. She had never been able to get along with her husband Mark, who demanded that she forego her career to stay at home, and after years of constant hostility, they separated. At first Susan was relieved that the conflict had ended, but soon she found herself lonely and depressed. She could not talk to her family, because they did not approve of her separation. She was embarrassed to discuss her situation with friends at church and soon dropped out. She told one friend, "I thought about talking to my minister, but he seemed so happily married, his wife such a model homemaker, that I just *knew* he couldn't understand. I decided to tough it out and just got more and more depressed."

Rabbi Earl A. Grollman makes a scathing indictment on the failure of clergy to help divorcing people:

> I believe that most clergy people are the wrong people to go to when someone has a problem such as dealing with divorce. I believe that too often the clergy can't handle the "trauma of divorce." They can't enter into the feelings of the person and therefore moralize and philosophize. Many, in fact, can't even handle their own marital problems.[1]

The irony, though, is that persons with marital difficulties often do turn to the clergy first for help. A 1979 survey by Richard A. Kulka and his associates at the University of Michigan shows that clergy head the list of physicians, psychiatrists, social workers, and others to whom troubled persons turn.[2] And it is not only church members who seek out the clergy when in need; numerous people in the community and those who belong to no church at all frequently turn to the clergy first for help. Their stigma seems less in their own eyes when they go to a member of the clergy rather than to a counselor. They perceive clergy as people who are trustworthy, usually available, and reasonably inexpensive.

If the present trend persists to legitimize and de-demonize divorce in the church, ministers can be expected to become increasingly involved in divorce counseling. However, clergy have not always responded with immediacy and attention to divorcing Christians. Often they find themselves like the man at midnight in one of Jesus' parables who said, "A friend of mine has arrived on a journey, and I have nothing to set before him" (Luke 11:6).

Some people, along with Tillich, believe that people turn away from the clergy in disappointment because many pastors have a self-righteous, pharisaic attitude. I believe, though, that people may perceive pastors as being unsympathetic or aloof simply because most ministers do not know what to do when someone in their parish experiences divorce. At times, pastors solve their dilemma by quick referral to marriage counselors. At other times they engage in the ritual drama of mutual pretense; both the divorcing persons and the clergy know what is happening, but they pretend it is not there, and the result of such pretending is all too obvious. When people experience the raw pain of a broken marriage, their minister is often either absent or ineffective. This situation must change in light of the unprecedented urgency of divorce. There are certain things that divorcing Christians should be able to expect from their minister.

Pastoral Care for the Divorcing

Theologian Daniel Day Williams has said, "The pastoral task, as it comes to every minister and every Christian, is to respond to the wonder of God's care for the soul and to share with others such knowledge as he has of God's healing power."[3] Whether the church is a positive or negative force in the lives of those experiencing divorce is largely determined by the minister and how the minister views his or her responsibility to such people. William A. Clebsch and Charles R. Jaekle have defined pastoral care as "helping acts, *done by representative Christian persons*, directed toward the *healing, sustaining, guiding,* and *reconciling* of *troubled persons* whose troubles arise *in the context of ultimate meanings and concerns.*"[4] Clergy have a total ministry to divorcing people which extends beyond the immediate crisis. As shepherds, they are to heal, sustain, guide, and be agents of reconciliation throughout the long divorce journey. As Robert Weiss points out, different stages in the divorce process present the individual with different coping tasks.[5] Clergy should be sensitive to these stages and should be aware what they can or cannot offer.

The decision-making phase begins with the breakdown of the relationship and the first consideration of separation, and ends with the decision to divorce and the act of physical separation. The restructuring stage begins with the physical separation, includes the hard work of mourning and redefining identity, and ends when the massive change is over and reconnection to life takes place.

Clergy need to be available at all of these crises. During the pre-divorce phase, their major role is to *guide* the couple into making the crucial decision whether to reinvent their marriage or to separate. During the divorcing stage, they need to *sustain* the couple and lead them to a mediated settlement. After the divorce, their responsibilities are to *heal* and to *be agents of reconciliation* as the couple work through their feelings about the broken marriage and begin the difficult task of discovering new beginnings.

The following is a simplified model of the divorce process, although it may vary slightly in some situations:

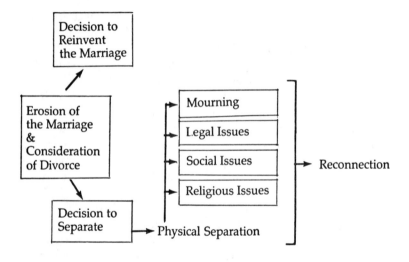

One aspect of the pastoral care of divorced persons by clergy is the role of divorce counseling. It is only recently that divorce

Counseling

One aspect of the pastoral care of divorced persons by clergy is the role of divorce counseling. It is only recently that divorce counseling has entered the helping professions. Emily M. Brown has said,

> Divorce counseling is a new phenomenon within the province of the helping professions. It is a recent adaptation of the society to the fact of divorce, and might be interpreted as the beginning of a significant change in the goals of the helping professions. Prevention of divorce has been a primary goal in dealing with marital problems, but divorce counseling implies that divorce is an acceptable option.[6]

Divorce counseling must be distinguished from divorce therapy. Therapy, as treatment for emotionally troubled people, involves in-depth analysis, usually in once-a-week sessions with a clinician. Counseling is assistance with normal problems in living; it offers guidance rather than treatment, and is educational, supportive, and oriented toward personal growth. The difference between therapy and counseling, though, is often more semantic than substantive. Divorce counseling certainly can be therapeutic and often involves using some of the classic models of therapy such as reality therapy, transactional analysis, or insight therapy. However, the divorce counselor should be able to distinguish between fairly well-adjusted people naturally upset by divorce and those who are severely disturbed. Clergy who practice divorce counseling should be aware of this distinction and be ready to make appropriate referral for those who need more intensive therapy. Some referral resources are listed in the notes.[7]

Stages of Divorce Counseling

Sheila Kessler has made distinctions between marriage counseling, limbo counseling, and divorce counseling.[8] Marriage counseling deals with problems in a marriage and focuses on the couple's staying together and reinventing their relationship. Effective marriage counseling helps the couple process their differences and reach workable solutions. Limbo counseling helps couples wrestle with the decision whether to divorce or not. Although one or both of the partners no longer want to invest their energies in the marriage, they have not yet decided to separate; there will be vacillation and changes of decision. Limbo counseling can be done either with couples or with the individual. Finally, divorce counseling begins when the decision to separate has been made, and it helps the couple to adjust until new life begins. Esther Fisher, one of the first to use the term *marriage and divorce counselor*, sets up three phases of such counseling: pre-divorce, during the divorce, and post-divorce.[9] Pre-divorce counseling concerns the imminent decision whether or not to divorce; divorce counseling deals with the legal process and lasts until a divorce is obtained; and post-divorce counseling involves helping people through emotional and practical problems after a divorce is finalized.

My plan for pastoral divorce counseling, which closely follows Fisher's model, also contains three major divisions: the *pre-divorce* phase, which focuses on the decision whether or not to divorce; the *divorcing* phase, which is concerned with litigation; and the *post-divorce* phase, in which issues of adjusting to the divorce are paramount.

Pastors as Counselors

Richard L. Krebs has recently argued that pastors should not be long-term counselors; rather, counseling by clergy should include only evaluation, support, and referral.[10] There can be brief and occasional pastoral conversations, but no in-depth pastoral counseling. Krebs cites as his reasons for this belief the following: (1) persons who come to ministers for counseling expecting instant success and quick personality change; (2) ministers who often transfer their own problems onto unsuspecting persons; (3) role confusion; and (4) misplaced priorities.[11]

On the other hand, David K. Switzer contends that the expectations placed on ministers by the pastoral role often make them the preferred and even the unique helper in a wide range of situations.[12] I believe divorce is one of those situations. Agreeing that few ministers are trained in the complexities of long-

MODEL FOR PASTORAL DIVORCE COUNSELING

	Pre-divorce Phase	*During Divorce Phase*	*Post-divorce Phase*
G O A L S	To help the couple decide whether or not to divorce.	To help the couple achieve a divorce settlement. (Structured Mediation)	To support and sustain both persons in adjusting to the divorce.
I N T E R V E N T I O N S	If both partners want to save the marriage, refer to marriage counseling. Offer alternative of structured separation. If divorce is the option, refer to divorce counseling.	Either be the mediator or refer to a lawyer skilled in divorce mediation.	Give supportive counseling to help the couple process feelings. Refer to Beyond Divorce Support Groups. Place divorce in a theological context, mediating forgiveness and facilitating repentance.

term counseling, Switzer nevertheless thinks that ministers ought to do crisis counseling, marriage counseling, and other kinds of counseling that involve problem-solving. He maintains,

> . . . he or she is called upon to include in legitimate pastoral care a response to the needs of persons in crisis, in grief, and persons with certain types of individual, marriage, and family problems which require more than an informal conversation and in which the minister may be the primary helping person, and, in some instances, the most effective helping person.[13]

Although it is true that ministers do not have the time to do long-term divorce counseling or to deal with severe emotional trauma caused by divorce, they can be the main helping person in the varying phases of the divorce process.

Pre-divorce Counseling

Pastoral initiative is crucial in pre-divorce counseling, because most church members who divorce withdraw and isolate themselves from the church during this time. Depressive withdrawal often deepens the feeling that no one cares. Divorcing people sometimes find they cannot muster up enough nerve to go to the minister for help. Some fear censure by clergy because of the stand taken against divorce by some churches. Ministers need to make themselves available by visiting families where marriages are in trouble and offering help. Other caring people in the congregation can also be helpful in suggesting that couples seek help from the minister. A couple may prefer to be seen conjointly by the pastor, or they may prefer to be seen individually, meeting together only occasionally. However, it is crucial that a couple have their first session with the minister together, for if one person is seen first, the other feels threatened and outnumbered.

These sessions always have a heated emotional climate, and the pastor may find it difficult to gain the confidence of both spouses, since each spouse may perceive the minister as taking the side of the other. If only one of the couple comes for counseling, great problems can arise; nonetheless, the minister can try to work with an individual and help process his or her feelings about separation.

One valuable tool for helping the minister assess where the couple stand in regard to separation is the Marital Status Inventory.[14] Although no such questionnaire can give a complete analysis of the intention to separate, the MSI does provide the minister with helpful information, because it can indicate, even before counseling begins, how close a relationship is to divorce, how ready each partner is to take the steps toward ending the marriage. The Inventory shows how the termination of a marriage unfolds as a series of discrete acts, from occasional thoughts about divorce to actually filing for divorce. The pastor may want to share the results of this inventory with the couple in order to see how accurate it is in evaluating their present feelings. It may also suggest the directions of the pre-divorce counseling sessions.

MARITAL STATUS INVENTORY

Circle True or False:

T—F   1. I have occasionally thought of divorce or wished that we were separated, usually after an argument or other incident.

T—F   2. I have considered divorce or separation a few times other than during or shortly after a fight, although only in vague terms.

T—F   3. I have thought specifically about separation or divorce. I have considered who would get the kids, how things would be divided, pros and cons of such actions, etc.

T—F   4. I have discussed the question of my divorce or separation with someone other than my spouse. (Trusted friend, psychologist, minister, etc.)

T—F   5. I have not suggested to my spouse that I wished to be divorced, separated or rid of him/her.

T—F   6. I have not made any specific plans to discuss separation or divorce with my spouse. I have not considered what I would say, etc.

T—F   7.   I have not discussed the issue seriously or at length with my spouse.

T—F   8.   My spouse and I have separated. [This is a (a) trial separation or (b) permanent separation. Check one.]

T—F   9.   Thoughts of separation or divorce occur to me very frequently, as often as once a week or more.

T—F   10.   I have made no inquiries from nonprofessionals as to how long it takes to get a divorce, grounds for divorce, costs involved in such action, etc.

T—F   11.   I have not consulted a lawyer or other legal aide about the matter.

T—F   12.   I have set up an independent bank account in my name as a measure of protecting my own interests.

T—F   13.   I have not contacted a lawyer to make preliminary plans for a divorce.

T—F   14.   I have filed for a divorce or we are divorced.

© Brunner/Mazel, 1980

It seems to me that there are four options for couples whose marriage is in trouble. They can let the marriage remain the way it is; they can decide to reinvent their marriage through marriage counseling; they can decide to separate; or they can decide on a structured separation.

If the couple are really unsure whether or not to divorce, structured separation is an option. Separation and divorce are not synonymous. Separation is a way of saying that one is uncertain; it is a temporary situation agreed to by a couple in order that they may decide more rationally whether or not to separate. Marjorie Kawin Toomin recommends a "structured separation with counseling" for such couples, a voluntary separation prior to a have-to separation, to help avoid manipulation and distrust.[15] Married couples meet individually and conjointly with their therapist during a three-month period in which they live apart and make no permanent financial, property, or child custody arrangements. When the predetermined time ends, the couple decide whether to live together permanently, live together on a time-limited trial basis, finalize the separation, or select a second period of structured separation. Of course, the danger of structured separation is that it amounts to a public announcement of the couple's difficulties. Sometimes the best "structured separation" is obtained by the time-honored tradition of temporarily sleeping in separate rooms, or by one partner's taking an extended trip alone.

During this pre-divorce counseling, the minister should keep two important rules in mind:

(1) *Never make decisions for the couple.* Ministers can bear burdens *with* divorcing people but not *for* them. J. C. Wynn emphasizes

> . . . we cannot make decisions for our people; that they must do for themselves. . . . To attempt to do so would put us in charge of their lives. We cannot do their work for them, believe for them, or shield them from the results of their actions. The detachment that is part of our professional stance prevents such interference in the lives of others, no matter how well-intended.[16]

The temptation will be for clergy to inject their own values about marriage or divorce in the counseling sessions. The minister should not be a protagonist for or against marriage, or for or against divorce, any more than he or she is for one spouse against the other. Sometimes, however, a couple considering separation may evoke feelings of anxiety, jealousy, or resentment in a minister who has a shaky marriage. Ministers who are themselves divorced may find that their own guilt over unresolved issues is triggered by the parishioners' divorce crisis, a situation which can prevent effective counseling.

If a minister has had no personal experience of divorce it can be difficult for him or her to allow anyone to give up completely on a marriage. On the other hand, a pastor already divorced and remarried may find it easy to be permissive about divorce and may encourage it prematurely. This is not to say that clergy should always keep their opinions about marriage and divorce to themselves, but when questioned by a couple in counseling, they should not state their values so dogmatically as to make the parishioners accept them as their own. The pastoral task is to guide the couple in making their own decisions. Some of the false assumptions that clergy maintain when couples come for pre-divorce counseling are: (1) reconciliation is always the preferred choice; (2) divorce is an unforgiveable sin and should be avoided at all costs; (3) divorce is always the best option for a troubled marriage; and (4) the spouse who is more reluctant to part and more committed to working on the marriage is the more mature and healthy one.

(2) Be careful of games couples play. Sometimes psychological games are played by couples who overtly seek counseling for their troubled relationship. If one of the couple has already decided to separate, he or she may view counseling as a token gesture or a way to assuage guilt. The minister is then seen as the "religious authority" who reinforces this decision. For example, a spouse wishing to disengage from a marital relationship feels guilty about leaving the family and goes for counseling to get help. If the other spouse begins a therapeutic alliance with the minister, the issue of guilt over abandonment is resolved. A woman once told me, "Please pastor, make my husband well, so I can leave him."

Pastors should be wary of being thrust into the role of marital rescuer. Invariably, one spouse will play the victim, with the mate as persecutor; he or she may then look to the pastor for rescue. Since there are no "innocent" or "guilty" parties in a divorce, however, the minister must remember that both persons are "victims" and "victimizers," and both share the responsibility for their broken marriage.

Sometimes the game "See How Hard I Tried" is played by one or both of the partners. One man, who obviously had decided on divorce even before beginning divorce counseling, glared with anger at his wife and said, "Look! I tried everything to make this marriage work, even counseling. So don't blame me." At other times, one or both of the couple play the game "Help Me" and expect the minister to save the marriage.

There is agony in making a decision about divorce. It is never easy, and it is rarely as amicable as some imply. Couples often flip-flop between separating and remaining in the marriage. The pastor needs to be there and help them look at all the alternatives, supporting whatever decision they make.

Divorce Mediation

Once the decision has been made to separate, the minister can sustain and guide the couple in the difficult process of working out a fair settlement. Norman Sheresky and Marya Mannes have said,

> So long as we continue to regard divorce as an arena in which one party bests the other, . . . unnecessary pain and anguish and the expenditure of unnecessary legal fees and costs will be the inevitable result.[17]

Despite many changes in recent years, divorce remains largely an adversary process in the eyes of the law, with one spouse being the "injured" party and the other the "guilty" party. Lawyers trained in this adversary system seem intent on attacking the interests of the other spouse. This is not the way Christians should divorce.

In 1978 O. J. Coogler developed a structured mediation model for divorce in which his goals were to help the couple reach their own responsible decisions about property settlement and child custody.[18] When the couple were involved in the total decision-making process, they had a greater ownership of the solution. Robert B. Coates outlines a form of divorce mediation that can be used by clergy, though it differs from secular divorce mediation in the way it sets goals:

(1) each party valuing the worth of the other as children of God,
(2) striving for fairness in negotiated outcome,
(3) placing above all else the welfare of the children by looking at the procedures through their eyes rather than only those of the parents,
(4) acknowledging the good experience of the past, mourning the loss, and forgiving one another,
(5) promoting an understanding of grace.[19]

In this style of mediation the minister acts as a neutral third party who does not decide the controversial issues, but encourages divorcing spouses to care for and cooperate with each other, while discouraging revenge-seeking. Granted, it might take further training in divorce negotiations, money management, tax law, divorce psychology, and counseling before the role of divorce mediator might well be assumed by clergy.

Clergy could also use *principled negotiation*, in which separating persons attack the problem, not each other. Often one spouse is a hard negotiator who views the separation as a contest of wills and is out to win at any cost. The other may be a soft negotiator who wants to avoid conflict and makes irrational concessions to "keep the peace." A good example of this conflict occurred when a husband blackmailed his wife into signing an unjust separation agreement by telling her, "If you sign this agreement, it will make it easier for me to come back." He had no intention of returning to the marriage. Roger Fisher and William Ury have said, ". . . in contrast to positional bargaining, the principled negotiation method of focusing on basic interests, mutually satisfying options, and fair standards typically results in a *wise* agreement."[20] Ministers can divert separating couples from further exacerbating their differences and can help them achieve a fair settlement. They can either refer couples to lawyers skilled in divorce mediation or can attempt to fill the mediating position themselves.

Post-divorce Counseling

People who decide to divorce are never really prepared for everything that follows. Even when there is some relief from the initial shock and pain, divorcing persons are barraged by a myriad of crises. Economic stress is a major problem, as suddenly there is a need to support two households rather than one, and the family income shrinks drastically. The embarrassment that ensues when the divorce becomes public, and the dissolving of the network of friends, create depression and loneliness. Some divorced people even become what Abigail Trafford calls "divorce flameouts," those who get stuck in one stage of the divorce process and stay stuck. Even under the best of circumstances, the post-divorce tranquillity is deceptively exhilarating and potentially dangerous. During this difficult time of coping with such a major change, the minister can be supportive in several different ways:

(1) Help process residual feelings about the divorce

Although strong feelings may erupt during the litigation phase, most couples are so intent on resolving these practical matters of children and property that they repress or deny their feelings for the moment. Later on, these unacknowledged feelings become all too present. The small death of divorce brings a mourning period that includes all the volatile emotions of grief: anger, denial, guilt, sadness, and depression. The minister can help separating people acknowledge these feelings. Often, in defense against the pain of loss, separating persons deny any hurt feelings and claim that they part as good friends. Also, some divorced persons experience extreme resentment when the other spouse remarries or finds a new life beyond divorce. They may feel a sense of injustice, especially if they believe that the newly prospering person was more guilty in causing the divorce. Others feel rejected and cannot escape the nagging suspicion that their former spouse's happy new life implies some guilt on their part.

Another common experience of some who divorce is the letdown that follows the brief euphoria. Anticipating a new freedom, if not a new life, many are not ready for the disappointment that follows separation. As one divorced man put it, "I felt released from one prison when I separated, but my single-again life was a new prison, even worse than before. I sometimes regretted my decision." Whatever strong feelings crop up after divorce—from the plethora of emotions that surround mourning, to post-divorce depression, to anger at a former spouse—the minister needs to be available to help people process them.

(2) Suggest a beyond divorce group

Such church-sponsored groups can play a crucial role in the recovery of divorced persons (See Chapter VI). If they are available, clergy should recommend them.

(3) Encourage full participation in the life of a church

The sad story of how some churches treat separated and divorced persons as second class citizens is all too evident. At times married people in the church even use discriminatory language, referring to divorced persons as "them" as opposed to "us." In some Protestant fundamentalist churches, divorced persons are allowed to sing in the choir, but not to sing solos. They can come to Sunday school, but not teach, and they are barred from being officers in the church. One wonders if there is any restriction in accepting their money! The pastor can help divorced persons find their place in the church. If they feel uncomfortable in the church because of the presence of the former spouse or because of any perceived rejection by the members, the pastor can help them relocate their membership. However, that decision is one they should make independently, not one they feel forced into by the polite avoidance or rejection of church members.

(4) Help work through the theological issues of divorce

This is a much-neglected aspect of divorce counseling; therapists and social workers are neither trained nor willing to explore the spiritual repercussions of divorce. Many church members believe that their divorce is an unforgivable sin, and they often feel abandoned by God and alienated from the church. As a spiritual director, the minister can help them to confess their own failures in the broken marriage, can mediate God's forgiveness, and can guide them into new life through repentance and reconciliation with former spouses. Janet Weinglass, Kenneth Kressel, and Morton Deutsch say that "Direct reassurance to clients about their freedom from guilt and their acceptability to God, as well as the catharsis of ritual confession are specifically religious interventions that have the effect of reducing emotional trauma."[21]

Preaching

Donald Capps has rightly shown that pastoral counseling and preaching should be integrated in a total ministry to persons.[22] There are several ways in which clergy can help divorced persons through the ministry of preaching:

(1) *Preaching can be pre-counseling activity.* People will probably know their pastor as a preacher before they have a chance to know him or her as a counselor. If the minister communicates from the pulpit that he or she is available for non-judgmental help when separation occurs, it might open the door for divorce counseling and divorce mediation. Many troubled people will seek out a pastor for counseling after the door has been opened for them in a sermon. If the humanness of ministers is evident, if they are perceived as being persons who have problems of their own, the way is open for separating/divorced persons to ask for help.

(2) *Sensitive preaching can educate the congregation about the church's response to divorce.* William Willimon tells about a friend of his who sought to resolve the relationship between counseling and preaching in his own ministry in regard to the problem of divorce.[23] Sermons dealing with the difficult passages about divorce in the New Testament (Matt. 19:3–12; Mark 10:1–12; Luke 16:18), as well as texts expounding the compassion of Christ for broken sinners (e.g., John 4:3–30; John 8:2–11), would foster a spirit of compassion and healing in the church. David Dalke, an ordained United Methodist minister, has created a model of divorce recovery based on the story of the liberation of the children of Israel in the book of Exodus.[24] All the great themes of the Exodus are present in the divorce journey of the Christian: bondage to a destructive relationship which thwarts and prevents growth, liberation, and the wilderness wanderings. The Israelites' fear of the unknown, their attempt to go back to Egypt, and their preference for the security of bondage over the dangers of the desert, well describe the journey of divorced people from bondage to freedom. And the final reward of the Israelites matches that of the successfully divorced: entry into the promised land of a new life.

Another rich biblical text for preaching on divorce and the Christian faith is the story of the disciples plucking ears of corn on the sabbath (Matt. 12:1–8; Mark 2:23–28; Luke 6:1–5). When the Pharisees take Jesus to task about this desecration of the sabbath, he reminds them how David entered the house of Abiathar the high priest and ate the bread of the Presence (Mark 2:26). Human need always takes precedence over law. Likewise, marriage was made for persons, not persons for marriage. Persons are far more precious and important than the institution of marriage.

The story of Peter's recovery of faith (Luke 22:31–34; John 21:15–19) might well describe the experience of divorce as people go through brokenness and failure and yet can be restored to new life. Also, the issue of whether Gentiles could be received as full members into the Christian church (Acts 10; Acts 15) could well be applied to the modern situation of accepting divorced people into the church, and thus the divorced persons could be seen as the "new Gentiles" of our contemporary world. Finally, some of the great Pauline passages about reconciliation and the church as the "family of God" could show how the church must embrace and support all of God's people if it is to be true to its divine calling (e.g., Eph. 2:11–22; 2 Cor. 5:15–21).

These are only a few passages which a minister could use in sermons to proclaim God's acceptance of the divorced person and enable the congregation to be compassionate toward their sisters and brothers who separate. Pastoral preaching that neither condones divorce nor condemns the divorced person might open doors for effective pastoral care for people undergoing divorce.

Whatever else the minister conveys to divorcing people, compassion is essential. Henri Nouwen has strong words to describe how modern professionalism in the clergy has often done away with Christlike compassion: The emphasis on skill training for clergy in the area of counseling is necessary. But the danger is that ministers will substitute analysis for compassion, and cease to be human. "But just as bread given without love can bring war instead of peace, professionalism without compassion will turn forgiveness into a gimmick, and the kingdom to come into a blindfold."[25] Nouwen's concept of clergy as wounded healers has special meaning for ministry to the divorced. Divorce is a painful, wrenching, death-like experience; what divorcing people need is sensitive, compassionate understanding. As Jesus said to the Pharisees of his day, "Go and learn what this means, 'I desire mercy, and not sacrifice.' For I came not to call the righteous, but sinners" (Matt. 9:13). Clergy who have themselves suffered and been healed, whether in divorce, loss through death, personal illness, or the loneliness of ministry, are potentially the wounded healers who may best care for divorced persons. Nouwen says of such clergy, ". . . a deep understanding of his [or her] own pain makes it possible for him [her] to convert . . . weakness into strength and to offer his [her] own experience as a source of healing to those who are often lost in the darkness of their own misunderstood sufferings."[26] Ministers' experience of brokenness and healing may be more valuable than any formal skills they possess.

Without doubt, clergy will encounter divorcing Christians who seek compassion, not condemnation. The responsibility—and the privilege—of a minister, is to offer them the kind of care that David R. Mace described over twenty-five years ago:

> Wherever there is human need, he [she] is pledged to do what lies in his [her] power to meet it. Condemnation or judgment of the divorced person, or self-righteous aloofness from his [her] distress, are unpardonable from a humane, let alone a Christian, point of view. In most instances, divorcing and divorced persons are the unhappy victims of our corporate blindness, stupidity, and neglect. They deserve and need both our sympathy and our succor. The great majority of them marry again; and if we deplore the fact that this first marriage failed, this should imbue us with zealous determination to enable them to ensure the success of their second attempt.[27]

VIII.
The Church
Reconstructs
Broken Lives

Why is it that when divorce strikes a family in the church, some kind of separation from the church has to happen? Sometimes both partners leave the church; sometimes one partner leaves, since it is too painful and embarrassing for both to be seen in the same church. But some divorced members never return to the church, either connecting with another church or remaining "outside the camp," like undesirable intruders. Must the church and the divorced continue to turn their backs on one another? Surely the agony of a broken marriage does not need to be compounded by the tragedy of a broken relationship with the church. It does not have to be this way.

These questions are all the more urgent since the church claims that it is a congenial fellowship of forgiven sinners, a spiritual family of brothers and sisters who have sinned and found the grace of God. One divorcée told me recently that she had remained in her church and even continued to attend the same young adult class as her former husband:

> In our church class, they accepted both of us and treated us as if nothing had changed. There were times when I looked across the room and saw Bob, and that hurt, but the class treated us as if we were members of a family. If it had not been for their love and concern, I might not have made it.

G. Edwin Bontrager has distinguished three major responses which the church makes to divorcing members. The first is a combination of hostility and standoffishness. Some members would prefer not to have persons around who are a threat to their ideas of marriage and religion. Second is tolerance, in which the church leaves the divorcing member(s) to find their own way and earn acceptance; they are tacitly required to "pay their dues" and work their way back into the good graces of the church whose standards they have offended. The third response—and the one often neglected—is intentional acceptance and affirmation.[1] The first two attitudes are in no way consistent with the spirit of Jesus Christ. On the contrary, they seem pointedly reminiscent of the pharisaic attitude which plagued Jesus in his ministry. The Christian church must find intentional ways to minister to divorced Christians if it is to maintain its integrity as the body of Christ.

Integrity of the Church at Stake

Simply put, how the church welcomes divorced members tests its integrity and the authenticity of its gospel. Divorced persons are the "new Gentiles" whose growing numbers cause the Christian church to struggle with the historical issue of welcoming sinners. Karl Heim has predicted, "The Church's future today depends more than ever on whether she withdraws into the ghetto and leaves the world to its fate, or whether she has the authority to continue the discussion with the world outside and to answer the questions which it puts to her."[2] There are too many divorced Christians in lonely spiritual ghettos for the church to be silent on this issue. Ministering to divorced Christians is one concrete way the church can "go forth to him outside the camp, bearing abuse for him" (Heb. 13:13).

(1) As the family of God

When Jesus was confronted by the crowd for not giving in to the demands of his mother and brothers who came to take him back to Nazareth (Mark 3:21), he looked at the disciples and said, "'Here are my mother and my brothers! Whoever does the will of God is my brother, and sister, and mother'" (Mark 3:34–35). In Jesus Christ, and in his body, the church, a new family exists based on true kinship with bonds much thicker than blood. This family consists of Christians who have known the heartbreak of separation and divorce, those who are widowed, . those parents whose children seem to have little concern for their welfare, and those children who seem alienated from their parents. This new family means that "you are no longer strangers and sojourners, but you are fellow citizens with the saints and members of the household of God" (Eph. 2:19).

The church needs to actualize this ideal of the family of God. Its average program is still geared to the traditional family. We speak of the family pew, family picnics, and family night suppers. There needs to be a new awareness of the entire church family. As Vande Kemp and Schreck put it,

> The church, as the redemptive community, comprises those people who know themselves on the basis of relationships restored. To God they stand in the relationship of children, fathered to spiritual life by his grace. To each other they are brothers and sisters, a relationship expressing the fact of their common Father. As such, these "consanguine" ties provide both the identity and belongingness of "family."[3]

Any overt or covert avoidance of divorced members, any attempt to herd them into "singles groups," is a denial of the nature of the church. Vande Kemp and Schreck go so far as to say,

> . . . the church's tendency to establish distinct organizations such as singles groups and "minister-to-singles" positions is suspect and constitutes an abdication of ministry by the church "family." . . . Singles groups in churches are little more than baptized "singles bars,"—incongruous reminders of how limited belongingness can be within the church, and how easily the church can be seduced into confusing group activity with genuine intimacy.[4]

It is a travesty that many mainline Protestant churches have either excluded singles from their inner circles or arranged for separate classes for them. Jürgen Moltmann gives some clear challenges to test whether the church makes its faith visible:

> that no one is left alone with his problems;
> that no one has to conceal his handicaps;
> that there is no one group of people who have the say about what is to be done, and another group who have no say;
> that neither old people nor children are isolated;
> that one person bears with the other, even if it is difficult and even when there is disagreement between them;
> that one person can leave another person in peace, if peace is what he needs.[5]

For those who have no family (or too much family), the church should offer a new family which embraces all regardless of merit or status. As Edwin Markham wrote,

> He drew a circle that kept me out,
> Rebel, heretic, a thing to flout;
> But love and I had the wit to win:
> We drew a circle that took him in.[6]

(2) As the reconciled fellowship

Lewis Rambo has said, "The church . . . is not a country club for the righteous but an emergency room for the critically injured and a hospital for those with an apparently terminal case of sin."[7] Just as the church needs to realize that life itself is terminal and that people with terminal illnesses should not be considered different, so divorced persons should be seen as no different from Christians who fail in other ways. Paul reminded the Galatians that good people can be "overtaken" and that there are no fail-safe Christians (Gal. 6:1). When people fail they need the support of the church, for all who have failed need grace.

Myrna and Robert Kysar sum up the church's duty of reconciliation:

> The aim . . . is that the asundered of our society might be reconciled—reconciled to God, the church, and to self. The ministry of the church must facilitate that reconciliation. . . . If the church can effectively communicate the fact of the reconciliation with God, it can also—as a community of faith—live a reconciled relationship with the divorced person.[8]

Reconciliation means reconciling divorced members not only to other church members, but to themselves, and to the former spouse. Even when reconciliation does not mean reuniting the marriage, it can mean a genuine concern that each partner get on with life.

Creative Liturgy and Learning

With awareness and guidance the church can ritualize divorce and remarriage. No doubt it will be easier to set new rituals for the latter than for the former; life is always easier to acknowledge than death. But since divorce is a small death, the church needs to be present. Walter Wangerin has said,

> Divorce is a death without a corpse. . . . It is not strange that the divorcing couple (unknowingly) tries to make of the court appearance a funeral—the participating ceremony of the community, some public support for them in their hour of need.[9]

The church needs to provide for divorcing people the possibility of a ritual such as the *Service of Divorce* in Chapter V. More and more the church is beginning to venture into the area of rituals for the divorcing, and I believe that they hold some promise for ministry to divorcing persons. Ministers should take the initiative in offering such services to those divorcing persons whom they counsel.

The presence of the congregation at a Christian remarriage is a way to ritualize the hope of resurrection beyond divorce.

Remarriages should not be private ceremonies but congregational acts, with all the celebration of first marriages if indeed "a third day" has occurred. The presence of the congregation is a visible sign to the couple that God's people stand with them as they begin a new life. It is a clear way for the congregation to say,

> We share our mutual woes; our mutual burdens bear
> And often for each other flows, the sympathizing tear.
> (John Fawcett, 1792).

Westerhoff and Willimon say that few pastoral issues have been avoided as much as divorce:

> "But we are recommending a program of catechesis that will help the whole church, children, youth, and adults, to understand the theological and moral, the psychological and social issues related to divorce so that the church might better minister to those persons and families in which there has been a divorce or one is contemplated."[10]

These intentional learning experiences should involve the whole church. I suggest that the minister and selected laity of the church offer a five-week, two-hour per week seminar on the subject *Divorce, Remarriage, and the Church*.

Seminars on Divorce, Remarriage
and the Church

Don S. Browning is correct when he says that the whole community of faith needs to be involved in caring for others in the church:

> Certainly the minister should counsel persons with marriage problems, sexual problems, and divorce problems, but he should first have helped to create among his people a positive vision of the normative meaning of marriage, sexuality, and even divorce.[11]

One strategy for creating a "positive vision" of divorce in the church is a series of seminars which are open to all members of the church. The following model has been found to be successful, although each church needs to create its own.

(1) Ground rules for participants

(A) Be good listeners. One danger of such seminars is that people will project their own experience of divorce on others. Some people may be reminded of their parents' divorce, and can ascribe their own unresolved feelings from the past to unsuspecting divorced people. Older couples may find the presence of a divorced person an occasion to recall the bitterness and hurt in the divorce of a son or daughter. Others may remember a time in their own marriage when they almost divorced, and they do not want to relive that pain. Worst of all, judgmental persons might cause further distress for the divorced by asking, "Why didn't you try harder to save your marriage?" It is crucial in such a seminar to *listen to others* without letting personal reactions get in the way.

(B) Be supportive, not judgmental.

(C) Accept differences of opinion and realize that each person's story *is* unique.

(D) Guard everyone's right to privacy.

(2) Session One

In preparation for the first session, distribute copies of *Is There Life After Divorce in the Church*. Ask all participants to read Chapter I. When the group gathers, meet in an informal setting, and sit in a circle.

(A) Make sure the participants are acquainted with each other. Since participation in the seminar is voluntary, ask the participants for the following information:

  name

  marital status

  concerns about this seminar

  expectations about the seminar

(B) Ask each participant to tell the group how he or she feels about divorce and remarriage.

(C) Discuss the myths and misconceptions in Chapter I, along with any other misconceptions about divorce which the group may mention.

(3) Session Two

(A) List on newsprint the stages of the divorce process, as outlined by Kessler, Bohannan, Trafford, and Morgan.
(B) Ask divorced members of the class if they would like to share their feelings about these stages and how they relate them to their own divorce journey.
(C) Compare how the church responds to "divorce grief" and "grief after death."
(D) Ask the participants to discuss whether Correu's stages of readiness for remarriage are also indications of "reconnection."

Assign Chapters III and IV for the next session.

(4) Session Three

(A) Have the participants describe different versions they have heard of what Jesus said about divorce and remarriage.
(B) Divide the group into five subgroups and ask each group to study one of the following biblical passages, relating the passage to the question of divorce:

> Mark 10:1–12: What did Jesus say about divorce and remarriage?
>
> Mark 2:23–28: How did Jesus contrast human law and human need?
>
> John 8:1–11: How does this story relate to divorced people & the church?
>
> 2 Corinthians 5:14–21: How does reconciliation occur for a divorced person?

(C) When the group reassembles, ask each subgroup to report its findings.
(D) Ask the participants to imagine that Jesus is in their midst and have them fantasize about what he would say today on divorce and remarriage.
(E) Ask the divorced persons in the group to comment on how their experience related to their faith.

Assign Chapter V to be read for the next session.

(5) Session Four

(A) Ask the divorced persons in the group to share the kinds of responses they received from church members when they first separated.

(B) Ask the married persons in the group to share how they felt when they first learned about a member's separation.

(C) Divide into pairs. Let one person roleplay a divorcing person and the other a church member, and practice avoiding "Mrs. Lincoln" responses.

(D) Ask the participants to discuss Henry T. Close's *Service of Divorce*.

(E) If any member of the group has participated in a Beyond Divorce Support Group, ask him or her to tell about it.

Assign Chapter VI to be read for the next session.

(6) Session Five

(A) Ask participants to imagine they are ministers and have been asked to perform a remarriage for members of the church. What would they do?

(B) Ask the group to discuss the *Ritual of Remarriage* and make suggestions for changing it.

(C) Propose three rounds of "fishbowl" discussions. In each round, several people are invited to join in a conversation in the center of the circle. Others sit in an outer circle and observe. (Allow 10 minutes or so for each round and provide an empty chair in the circle for anyone who wants to join the discussion).

First, invite all biological parents into the fishbowl and ask them to discuss the problems of disciplining their children. Identify the problems and discuss strategies.

Second, invite all single parents into the fishbowl to discuss the same issue.

Third, do the same for all stepparents.

Fourth, do the same for "hybrid parents," i.e., those who have both biological children and stepchildren.

(D) When the group reassembles, discuss the differences (if any) in discipline in the different types of families.

It might be effective to close the seminar with a worship service celebrating the unity of the church and praising God for the "new family" of brothers and sisters in Jesus Christ.

Being a People-oriented Shepherd

One of the major issues about ministry to divorced parents is whether or not to develop a specialized ministry. My belief is that at the early stages of separation, when the pain is most intense and divorcing persons perceive rejection from other church members, a Beyond Divorce Support Group is helpful. However, divorcing Christians should never be segregated from the rest of the congregational life at this time and should never be identified as "different" by other church members.

In the truest sense, the congregation itself should be the shepherd, caring for the divorced. William Oglesby gives the following broad definition of pastoral care:

> In the biblical sense, pastoral care is that function of the people of God wherein we "bear one another's burdens, and so fulfill the law of Christ" (Gal. 6:2) as the means for participating in the process of reconciliation. . . . It is a process whereby we listen with gentleness and patience, speak with truth and love, hold out a hand in time of loneliness and fear, sit in silence through the long night watches, and rejoice when the shadow of distress is dissolved in the warm sun of deliverance.[12]

This means that the congregation become lay caregivers and no longer expect the clergy to do all the "ministering" by themselves. Diane Detwiler-Zapp and William Caveness Dixon show how existing groups within the church can become effective caregiving groups, and how new groups, such as a Divorce Support Group, can be used to meet the needs of parishioners.[13] Howard W. Stone has prepared an excellent step-by-step guide to help clergy train lay people in pastoral care.[14] The principles outlined in this book and tested by the author in various churches successfully build the strengths that lay people need to become effective caregivers and to refine their abilities in the ministry of healing, sustaining, guiding, and reconciling.

When divorcing persons first experience the overwhelming emotions of separation, they need people to listen. Lewis Rambo has said,

Those who minister to the divorced should realize the person may have an insatiable appetite to tell the tale over and over again. This phenomenon of repetition seems to be one way of doing the work of disconnecting. The divorcing person will seek to understand the catastrophic event by repeating the trauma again and again. The person cannot *not* repeat the story. The person feels compelled or driven somehow to come to terms with the awful event.[15]

While it is true that those who have gone through divorce may be best suited to help someone in that situation, a person does not have to be involved in a marriage coming apart at the seams to understand one that is. Nouwen is right when he says that there is great power in sharing our wounded being with another; wounds can become a source of healing. ". . . wounds and pain become openings or occasions for a new vision," Nouwen affirms. They ". . . are transformed from expressions of despair into signs of hope."[16]

The congregation is called to care for the divorced. No word or act can really alleviate the pain and sorrow that must be lived through, nor would the divorced want church members to do that. However, words and actions do let them know that they are not alone, that the church cares. What great potential for compassion exists in the congregation of the faithful!

Offering Koinonia

Some time ago I participated in a closing worship service in a large Presbyterian church. We joined hands as "the family of God" and sang, "Blest Be the Tie That Binds Our Hearts in Christian Love." But as I glanced around the room I saw none of the singles of the church, save a few widows; I saw families. I felt as if I were attending a family reunion instead of a church. How much more would we have affirmed the nature of the church if single parents, children from single-parent homes, and divorced persons were present! Those people especially needed the closeness and warmth we all felt. The Psalmist exclaimed, "Even the sparrow finds a home, and the swallow a nest for herself, where she may lay her young, at thy altars, O LORD of hosts, my King and my God" (Ps. 84:3). This is what the church needs to provide for those deprived of home by divorce: a spiritual home. At the conclusion of a Beyond Divorce Support Group, one of the members read this passage from Thomas R. Kelly's *A Testament of Devotion* and thanked the group for being her new family:

> Within the wider Fellowship emerges the special circle of a few on whom, for each of us, a particular emphasis of nearness has fallen. These are our special gift and task. . . . The total effect, in a living Church, would be sufficient intersection of these bonds to form a supporting, carrying network of love for the whole of mankind. Where the Fellowship is lacking the Church invisible is lacking and the Kingdom of God has not yet come.[17]

That is the experience of koinonia, the fellowship which divorced persons should find in the church. Merely providing a class for singles or occasional "mix and match" social gatherings is not enough. Vande Kemp and Schreck emphasize,

> Without access to intimate inclusion, the church's response to the single who is lonely, disconnected, and unsure of his personal identity and worth is hypocritical. A singles group cannot take the place of invitations to homes, inclusion in familial and cross-generational activities, and the mutual sharing of non-single experiences of life.[18]

The following story, told by John Slyker, points the way for the church to include divorced persons:

> Members of our class wanted to form a Sunday School class to meet the needs of unattached adults. We felt that the name of the class should reflect contemporary life styles. "Young Adults" was rejected, as age wasn't a consideration. Anything to do with "singles" seemed inappropriate because an unattached person might marry and want to stay in the class with friends. And so it went for 45 minutes, until no one had any ideas left. Moments of silence passed. Then one man's face lit up. Smiling, he said, "Why don't we call it 'Come as You Are'?"[19]

If the church is koinonia, then the pain of one member affects the whole church. "If one member suffers, all suffer together" (1 Cor. 12:26). For divorced Christians, the church must be the shepherd and offer the kind of community which cannot be found in the secular world.

Monica J. Maxon tells about a friend named Sylvia who went through a divorce. "She and her husband were both deeply committed to their nearby church community, but when he left her and their two small children, she went to one worship service, then could not continue. Those who had been her Christian companions talked about her, she said, not to her. She preferred to stay at home."[20] Sylvia's story is typical. Maxon comments,

> She needed to feel stronger before she could return. Unfortunately, that feeling is all too common. Instead of going to the community when in despair, we wait; we gather our resources outside the community. The grieving person puts up a good front for the church, but no real sharing occurs.[21]

This book has described how churches approach divorcing members in one of three ways. Some churches are extremely negative toward divorce and let that attitude cause rejection of divorced members; those who get divorced, with few exceptions, are spiritual deviants and unforgivable sinners. A second response, perhaps the predominant one, is to deny the reality and pretend that the divorce is not taking place. The divorce may also be condoned and treated lightly, without regard for the participants' pain and grief. Finally, there is polite silence; when the separation occurs, no one calls to inquire about the divorcing person and his or her family. There are also subtle rejections, like being left out of social happenings and forgotten in congregational life and work.

None of these responses reflects the spirit of Jesus Christ or is at all compatible with his true church. Divorce is a major crisis for any person, but especially for a Christian. What happens in the complexity of a relationship between husband and wife cannot really be understood by people on the outside. John Milton quotes a Roman who, when asked why he put away his wife, pulled off his shoe and said, "This shoe is a neat shoe, yet none of you know where it wrings me."[22] Since no one can really know how people can be wrung by a destructive marriage, no one should judge or condemn. Divorce can elicit only one Christian response: the kind of strong compassion that helps divorced persons find new life. This new life demands hard work, but it begins with the experience of grace.

There can be a "third day" for divorcing Christians who undergo the death of a marriage. The church needs to proclaim that those who have allowed a part of their life to die can welcome resurrection and can begin again. There *can* be life after divorce in the church. Isaiah's words to the exiles are prophetic for divorced persons:

"Remember not the former things,
    nor consider the things of old.
Behold, I am doing a new thing;
    now it springs forth, do you not perceive it?"
                                        (Isa. 43:18–19)

Milton was right when he said, "What a violent and cruel thing it is to force the continuing of those together whom God and nature in the gentlest end of marriage never joined."[23] It will be "the third day" in the church when the divorced find grace instead of rejection, and truth instead of denial. The church cannot bear the burden for divorced persons; no one would expect that. It can, however, share the burden with them, and that is one reason why it exists.

There is therefore now
no condemnation
for those who are in Christ Jesus.
                    (Rom. 8:1)

Notes

I. A Nagging Issue: Divorced Persons in the Church

1. William V. Arnold et al., *Divorce: Prevention or Survival* (Philadelphia: The Westminster Press, 1977), 57. Reprinted by permission.
2. Vidal S. Clay, "Where Are the Neighbors Bringing in Food?" *Pilgrimage* 3 (Summer 1975): 36, 37.
3. See Willard Waller, *Old Love and the New: Divorce and Readjustment* (Carbondale, Ill.: Southern Illinois University Press, 1958) and Ernest R. Grove, *Conserving Marriage and the Family: A Realistic Discussion of the Divorce Problem* (New York: Macmillan, 1944).
4. Margaret Mead, "Doubletalk About Divorce," *Redbook Magazine* 131 (May 1968): 47.
5. William B. Oglesby, Jr., "Divorce and Remarriage in Christian Perspective," *Pastoral Psychology* 25 (4) (Summer 1977): 283. Copyright © 1977 by Human Sciences Press, 72 Fifth Avenue, New York, N.Y. 10011. Reprinted by permission.
6. Dory Krongelb Beatrice, "Divorce: Problems, Goals, and Growth Facilitation," *Social Casework* 60 (March 1979): 158.
7. Robert F. Sinks, "A Theology of Divorce," *The Christian Century* 94 (April 20, 1977): 379. Copyright 1984 Christian Century Foundation. Reprinted by permission from the April 20, 1977 issue of *The Christian Century*.
8. Stephen J. Kelleher, "The Laity, Divorce, and Remarriage," *Commonweal* 102 (November 7, 1975): 524.
9. Andrew J. Cherlin, *Marriage, Divorce, Remarriage: Social Trends in the United States* (Cambridge, Mass.: Harvard University Press, 1981), 29.
10. Paul Bohannan, "The Six Stations of Divorce," in *Divorce and After* ed. Paul Bohannan (Garden City, N.Y.: Doubleday and Company, 1971), 48.
11. Edmund Bergler, *Divorce Won't Help* (New York: Liveright Publishing Company, 1978), vii.
12. Abigail Trafford, *Crazy Time: Surviving Divorce* (New York: Harper and Row, 1982), 67.
13. Esther Oshiver Fisher, *Divorce: The New Freedom* (New York: Harper and Row, 1974), 16.
14. Thomas H. Holmes and Richard H. Rahe, "The Social Readjustment Rating Scale," *Journal of Psychosomatic Research* 2 (August 1967): 213–18.

15. E. Mavis Hetherington, Martha Cox, and Roger Cox, "Divorced Fathers," *Psychology Today* 10 (April 1977): 46.
16. Bruce Fisher, *Rebuilding: When Your Relationship Ends* (San Luis Obispo, Calif.: Impact Publishers, 1981), 51.
17. Mel Krantzler, *Creative Divorce* (New York: New American Library, 1975), 29.
18. Hetherington, Cox, and Cox, "Divorced Fathers," 46.
19. Lewis R. Rambo, *The Divorcing Christian* (Nashville: Abingdon Press 1983), 16. Reprinted by permission.
20. Lyle E. Schaller, "Clergy Divorced Are More Accepted," *Religious News Service* (March 18, 1982): 34.
21. Howard J. Clinebell, Jr., *The Mental Health Ministry of the Local Church* (Nashville: Abingdon Press, 1962), 205.
22. Hendrika Vande Kemp and G. Peter Schreck, "The Church's Ministry to Singles: A Family Model," *Journal of Religion and Health* 20 (Summer 1981): 153. Copyright © 1981 by Human Sciences Press, Inc., 72 Fifth Avenue, New York, N.Y. 10011.
23. Elaine Tyler May, *Great Expectations: Marriage and Divorce in Post-Victorian America* (Chicago: University of Chicago Press, 1980), 163.
24. Wayne E. Oates, *The Christian Pastor* (Philadelphia: The Westminster Press, 1964), 26. Reprinted by permission.

II. Loosening the Tie That Binds: Pain and Process

1. Ronald D. Laing, *The Politics of Experience* (New York: Pantheon Books, 1967).
2. Sheila Kessler, *The American Way of Divorce: Prescriptions for Change* (Chicago: Nelson-Hall, 1975), 1.
3. Ibid., 20.
4. Bohannan, "The Six Stations of Divorce," 33–62.
5. Donald J. Froiland and Thomas L. Hozman, "Counseling for Constructive Divorce," *The Personnel and Guidance Journal* 55 (May 1977): 525–29.
6. Trafford, *Crazy Time*.
7. Ibid., 169.
8. Robert S. Weiss, *Marital Separation* (New York: Basic Books, 1975), 48. Copyright © 1975 Basic Books, Inc.
9. See Robert S. Weiss, *Loneliness: The Experience of Emotional and Social Isolation* (Cambridge, Mass.: MIT Press, 1973) and Morton and Bernice Hunt, *The Divorce Experience* (New York: New American Library, 1979).
10. Bohannan, "The Six Stations of Divorce," 37.
11. Silvano Arieti, "Roots of Depression: The Power of the Dominant Other," *Psychology Today* 12 (April 1979): 92.
12. Waller, *Old Love*, 135.

13. Albert Camus, *The Plague*, trans. Stuart Gilbert (New York: Alfred A. Knopf, 1969), 66. Copyright © Reprinted by permission of Alfred A. Knopf, Inc.
14. Carl E. Braaten, "Sex, Marriage and the Clergy," *Dialog: A Journal of Theology* 18 (Summer 1979): 174.
15. Ira W. Hutchison and Katherine R. Hutchison, "The Impact of Divorce Upon Clergy Career Mobility," *Journal of Marriage and the Family* 41 (November 1979): 847–60.
16. John C. Morgan, "The Divorce: In the Court; In the Pastor's Study," Copyright ©. Reprinted by permission of John C. Morgan.
17. Hetherington, Cox, and Cox, "Divorced Fathers," 45.
18. Alvin Toffler, *Future Shock* (New York: Random House, 1970), 236–59; 371–97.
19. Reva S. Wiseman, "Crisis Theory and the Process of Divorce, *Social Casework* 56 (April 1975): 212.
20. Friedrich Nietzsche, *Twilight of the Idols and the Anti-Christ*, trans. R. J. Hollingdale, Jr. (New York: Penguin Books, 1969), 120.
21. Larry M. Correu, *Beyond the Broken Marriage* (Philadelphia: The Westminster Press, 1982), 118–119.
22. "How Heavy the Days" from POEMS by Hermann Hesse, selected and translated by James Wright. (New York: Farrar, Straus and Giroux, 1970), 43. Copyright © 1970 by James Wright. Reprinted by permission of Farrar, Straus and Giroux, Inc.
23. Hermann Hesse, from "Stages" in *The Glass Bead Game*, trans. Richard and Clara Winston (New York: Holt, Rinehart, and Winston, 1969), 444. Copyright © 1969. Reprinted by permission of Holt, Rinehart, & Winston.

III. "'Tis All in Pieces": The Need for a Christian Theology of Divorce

1. Stephen J. Kelleher, "The Problem of the Intolerable Marriage," *America* 119 (September 14, 1968): 178–82.
2. Kelleher, *Divorce and Remarriage for Catholics?* (New York: Doubleday, 1973), 179.
3. See James J. Young, ed., *Growing Through Divorce* (Ramsey, N.J.: Paulist Press, 1981); Paula Ripple, *The Pain and the Possibility: Divorce and Separation Among Catholics* (Notre Dame, Ind.: Ave Maria Press, 1978); and Kevin T. Kelly, *Divorce and Second Marriage: Facing the Challenge* (New York: The Seabury Press, 1983).
4. Les Woodson, *Divorce and the Gospel of Grace* (Waco, Tex.; Word Books, 1979), 24.
5. *The Christian Century* 101 (January 4–11, 1984):10.
6. Robert E. Elliott, "A Theology of Divorce," *Perkins Faculty Symposium* (Dallas, Tex., 1975–1976): 1.

7. Nelson Manfred Blake, *The Road to Reno* (New York: Macmillan, 1962), 11. Copyright © Nelson M. Blake 1962. Reprinted by permission.

8. Charles C. Ryrie, "Biblical Teaching on Divorce and Remarriage," *Grace Theological Journal* 3 (1982): 191–92.

9. See Myrna and Robert Kysar, *The Asundered: Biblical Teachings on Divorce and Remarriage* (Atlanta: John Knox Press, 1978).

10. Arnold et al., *Divorce*, 55.

11. Donald W. Shaner concludes that Luke 16:18 gives the original teaching (with slight modification from Mark 10:12). He states, "The parallel passage, Matthew 5:32, is a conflation of Q with Mark 10:11–12. Matthew 19:9 is drawn directly from Mark 10:11." See also Donald W. Shaner, *A Christian View of Divorce According to the Teachings of the New Testament* (Leiden, Netherlands: E. J. Brill, 1969), 107.

12. Keith Rayner, "Marriage After Divorce: Some Theological Considerations," *St. Mark's Review* (September 1983): 2–7.

13. Ibid., 5.

14. Ibid., 6.

15. Dwight Hervey Small, *The Right to Remarry* (Old Tappan, N.J.: Fleming H. Revell, 1977), 28.

16. John B. Cobb, Jr., *Theology and Pastoral Care* (Philadelphia: Fortress Press, 1977), 40

17. *Divorce and Remarriage with Special Reference to Ordained Ministers* (Atlanta: Office of the Stated Clerk, 1978), 7.

18. James G. Emerson, Jr., *Divorce, the Church, and Remarriage.* (Philadelphia: The Westminster Press, 1961), 11–32.

19. Sinks, "A Theology of Divorce," 379.

20. Ibid., 377–78.

21. Joseph Fletcher, *Situation Ethics: The New Morality* (Philadelphia: The Westminster Press, 1966), 133.

22. Thomas M. Olshewsky, "A Christian Understanding of Divorce," *Journal of Religious Ethics* 7 (Spring 1979): 127.

23. Ibid., 128.

24. Sandra Read Brown, "Clergy Divorce and Remarriage," *Pastoral Psychology* 30 (Spring 1982): 191. Copyright © 1982 by Human Sciences Press, 72 Fifth Avenue, New York, N.Y. 10011. Used by permission.

25. Ibid., 192.

26. T. Craig Weaver, "A Niebuhrian View of Divorce," Master's thesis, Wake Forest University, 1982, v–vi.

27. Ibid., vi.

28. *The Constitution and Canons of the Episcopal Church*, Title I, Canon 18, Section 2.

29. Philip Turner, "The Marriage Canons of the Episcopal Church: (I) Scripture and Tradition," *Anglican Theological Review* 65 (October 1983): 371–83.
30. Ibid., 372.
31. Turner, "The Marriage Canons of the Episcopal Church: (II) The Case from Reason," *Anglican Theological Review* 66 (January 1984): 19.
32. *Westminster Confession of Faith*, Presbyterian Church, U.S.A., Section 2, 1953.
33. *Westminster Confession of Faith*, Presbyterian Church, U.S., 1969 version. Chapter XXVI, p. 6, paragraph 109.
34. 2 Sam. 12:13; Neh. 9:17; Ps. 32:5; 130:4; Matt. 12:13a; 21:31,32; Luke 7:36–50; 15:11–32; John 3:16, 17; 8:3,11; Rom. 3:23; 10:9,10; Gal. 6:1; 1 Tim. 2:4; Heb. 7:25; 1 John 1:9, 2:1,2.
35. Presbyterian Church, U.S. *Book of Church Order*, 1978–1979 ed., 215–6.
36. Minutes of the Ninety-eighth General Assembly of the Presbyterian Church, U.S. (Part I, 1958), p. 44, 188–191.
37. Quoted in James P. Lichtenberger, *Divorce: A Study in Social Causation* (New York: Columbia University Press, 1909).
38. *The Book of Discipline*, United Methodist Church (Nashville: United Methodist Publishing House, 1939), 194.
39. *Doctrine and Discipline of the United Methodist Church* (Nashville: United Methodist Publishing House, 1964), 159, 666ff.
40. *The Book of Discipline*, United Methodist Church, (Nashville: United Methodist Publishing House, 1976, 1980, 1984), par. 71–C, 89.
41. Janis Johnson, "Religion Comes to Terms with Divorce," *USA Today* (December 29, 1983): 3D.
42. Donald G. Miller, *The Biblical Doctrine of Marriage*, unpublished manuscript (Richmond, Va.: Union Theological Seminary, 1953), 1.
43. Ibid., 6.
44. Ernest Trice Thompson, "The Bible, Our Church and Divorce and Remarriage," *The Presbyterian Outlook* 135 (July 13, 1953): 4.
45. Ibid.
46. Ibid.,5.

IV. A Christian Theology of Divorce

1. John Milton, *Colasterion* (1643). In *The Doctrine and Discipline of Divorce*, Milton argued that (1) divorce ought to be allowable on the grounds of incompatibility; (2) legal permission for divorce ought to be granted on the grounds of mutual agreement by the petitioning spouses.
2. Martin Bucer, *De Regno Christi* (1550). Bucer argued that when the union between husband and wife was absent, no marriage existed, and divorce was permissible.

3. Lewis R. Smedes, "Divorce: An Ethical Response" *The Reformed Journal* 26 (October 1976): 11–12.
4. William H. Willimon, *Saying YES to Marriage* (Valley Forge, Pa.: Judson Press, 1979), 91–92.
5. *The Book of Common Prayer*, Protestant Episcopal Church in America (1976 edition), 429.
6. Robert Farrar Capon, *A Second Day: Reflections on Remarriage*. (New York: William Morrow and Company, 1980), 152–53. See also Walter Wangerin, "On Mourning the Death of a Marriage," *Christianity Today* 28 (May 18, 1984): 20–23.
7. Turner, "Marriage Canons (II)," 13.
8. Jill Morgan, *This Was His Faith: The Expository Letters of G. Campbell Morgan* (New York: Fleming H. Revell, 1952), 294.
9. Oates, *Pastoral Counseling* (Philadelphia: The Westminster Press, 1974), 219. Reprinted by permission.
10. Karl Barth, *On Marriage* (Philadelphia: Fortress Press, 1968), 41.
11. Rambo, *The Divorcing Christian*, 27–28.
12. Capon, *A Second Day*, 37.
13. Ibid.
14. Henri J. M. Nouwen, *The Living Reminder: Service and Prayer in Memory of Jesus Christ* (New York: The Seabury Press, 1979), 17.
15. Rosemary Ruether, "Divorce: No Longer Unthinkable," *Commonweal* 86 (April 14, 1967): 122.
16. Olshewsky, "A Christian Understanding of Divorce," 128.
17. S. Brown, "Clergy Divorce and Remarriage," 194.
18. Kysar, *The Asundered*, 104.
19. Emerson, *Divorce, the Church, and Remarriage*, 166.
20. Carroll A. Wise, *Pastoral Psychotherapy: Theory and Practice* (New York: Jason Aronson, 1980), 292.
21. Paul Tillich, *The New Being* (London: SCM Press, 1956), 24.
22. Elizabeth Cauhapé, *Fresh Starts: Men and Women After Divorce* (New York: Basic Books, 1983).
23. S. Brown, "Clergy Divorce and Remarriage," 194.
24. Ernest Hemingway, *A Farewell to Arms* (New York: Charles Scribner's Sons, 1929), 249.
25. Thomas C. Oden, *The Structure of Awareness* (Nashville: Abingdon Press, 1969), 23–24.
26. Sinks, "A Theology of Divorce," 378.
27. Martin Luther, August 1, 1521. Letter 91 in *Luther's Works*, Vol. 48 (Philadelphia: Fortress Press, 1955), 281–2.
28. Barth, *On Marriage*, 41.
29. Thomas S. Kuhn, *The Structure of Scientific Revolutions* (Chicago: University of Chicago Press, 1962).
30. Arnold et al., *Divorce*, 57.

31. Gerald F. Jacobson, *The Multiple Crises of Marital Separation and Divorce* (New York: Grune and Stratton, 1983).
32. Mitchell Salem Fisher, *Rebel, O Jews!* (New York: Reconstructionist Press, 1973), 24. Copyright © M. S. Fisher. Reprinted by permission of Reconstructionist Press.

V. The Church Responds to Initial Pain

1. John H. Westerhoff III and William H. Willimon, *Liturgy and Learning Through the Life Cycle* (New York: The Seabury Press, 1980), 121.
2. Elliott, "A Theology of Divorce," 16.
3. Oates, *Pastoral Care and Counseling in Grief and Separation* (Philadelphia: Fortress Press, 1976), 76.
4. Westerhoff and Willimon, *Liturgy and Learning*, 121.
5. A. S. Maller, "A Religious Perspective on Divorce," *Journal of Jewish Communal Service* 55 (1978): 192–94.
6. Phyllis Jean Sedgwick Flowers, from a worship service at Edgehill Methodist Church, Nashville, Tennessee. The service is found in Eugene C. Holmes, ed., *Ritual in a New Day* (Nashville: Abingdon Press, 1976), 88–90.
7. Ibid., 90.
8. For examples see the following rituals: Sam R. Norman, "A Ceremony for the Divorced," *The Journal of Pastoral Care* 33 (March 1979): 60–63; Ruth Meagher and David Voss, "An Unsacrament for a Broken Covenant," *Pilgrimage* 3 (Fall-Winter, 1975): 1–4; Mary McDermott Shideler, "An Amicable Divorce," *Christian Century* 88 (May 5, 1971): 553–55. An Episcopal ceremony, written by Episcopal priest David H. Benson and therapist Sherrill H. Skyol, is found in Westerhoff and Willimon, *Liturgy and Learning*, 124–29. A Roman Catholic ritual appears in *Handbook of Family Therapy*, ed. Alan S. Gurman and David P. Kniskern (New York: Brunner/Mazel, 1981): 689–90.
9. David Ulrich, Frederick Bender, and Faith Whitfield, *A Service of Affirmation When Parents Are Separating* (Cincinnati: Forward Movement Publications, 1982).
10. Ibid., 8.
11. Gurman and Kniskern, *Handbook*, 690.
12. Henry T. Close, "A Service of Divorce," *Pilgrimage* 5 (Spring 1977): 61. Copyright © Henry T. Close. Reprinted by permission of Human Sciences Press.
13. Ibid., 60–64.
14. Weiss, *Marital Separation*, 156. Copyright © Basic Books, Inc.
15. Ibid., 158–59.
16. John R. Landgraf, *Creative Singlehood and Pastoral Care* (Philadelphia: Fortress Press, 1982), 59.

17. Brooke B. Collison, "The Mrs. Lincoln Response," *The Personnel and Guidance Journal* 57 (December 1978): 180.
18. Dietrich Bonhoeffer, *Life Together*, trans. John W. Doberstein (New York: Harper and Row, 1954), 97.
19. For further help with Divorce Support Groups see the following: LeRoy J. Spaniol and Paul A. Lannan, *Getting Unstuck: Moving on After Divorce* (Ramsey, N.J.: Paulist Press, 1984); B. Fisher, *Rebuilding*; William Bridges, *Transitions: Making Sense of Life's Changes* (Reading, Mass.: Addison-Wesley, 1982); Sheila Kessler, "Divorce Adjustment Groups," *The Personnel and Guidance Journal* 54 (January 1976): 251–55; and Sara E. Bonkowski and Brenda Wanner-Westly, "The Divorce Group: A New Treatment Modality," *Social Casework* 60 (November 1979): 552–57.
20. See James J. Young, ed. *Ministering to the Divorced Catholic* (Ramsey, N.J.: Paulist Press, 1979) and Ripple, *The Pain and the Possibility*.
21. Matthew Fox, *A Spirituality Named Compassion and the Healing of the Global Village: Humpty Dumpty and Us.* (Minneapolis, Minn.: Winston Press, 1979), 49.
22. Kessler, "Divorce Adjustment Groups," 253.
23. Paul W. Pruyser, *The Minister as Diagnostician* (Philadelphia: The Westminster Press, 1976), 60–79.
24. Thomas Moore, "Come, Ye Disconsolate," 1816. From *The Hymnbook* (Richmond, Philadelphia, and New York: Presbyterian Church in the United States, The United Presbyterian Church in the U.S.A., and the Reformed Church in America, 1955), 373.
25. Excerpt from the WOUNDED HEALER by Henri Nouwen. Copyright © 1972 by Henri J. M. Nouwen. Reprinted by permission of Doubleday & Company, Inc., 71–2.

VI. The Church Responds to Life After Divorce

1. Oates, *Pastoral Counseling*, 229.
2. See Sharon Price-Bonham and Jack O. Balswick, "The Noninstitutions: Divorce, Desertion, and Remarriage," *Journal of Marriage and the Family* 42 (November, 1980): 959–72.
3. Cherlin, *Marriage, Divorce, Remarriage*, 91.
4. The reader should consult such books as Raymond Kay Brown, *Reach Out to Singles: A Challenge to Ministry* (Philadelphia: The Westminster Press, 1979); William Lyon, *A Pew for One, Please: The Church and the Single Person* (New York: The Seabury Press, 1977); and Landgraf, *Creative Singlehood* for excellent treatments of the church's ministry to single-again persons.
5. Stanley A. Ellisen, *Divorce and Remarriage in the Church* (Grand Rapids, Mich.: Zondervan, 1980), 16–17.
6. Oates, "The Church, Divorce, and Remarriage," *Review and Expositor* 61 (Spring 1964): 45–60.

7. See, for example, John Murray, *Divorce* (Grand Rapids, Mich.: Baker Book House, 1961) and J. R. W. Stott, *Divorce* (Downer's Grove, Ill.: Inter-Varsity Press, n.d.).

8. Oglesby, "Divorce and Remarriage," 291.

9. Gordon Wenham, "May Divorced Christians Remarry?" *Churchman* 95 (1981): 160.

10. David Atkinson, *To Have and to Hold: The Marriage Covenant and the Discipline of Divorce* (Grand Rapids, Mich.: William B. Eerdmans Press, 1979), 191.

11. Dorothy Cantor, "Divorce: Separation or Individuation?" Paper presented at the Annual Meeting of the APA, Los Angeles, California, 1981.

12. George W. Knight, *The Second Marriage Guidebook* (Brentwood, Tenn.: J. M. Publications, 1983).

13. Ibid.

14. Laura Singer with Barbara Lang Stern, *Stages: The Crises That Shape Your Marriage* (New York: Grosset and Dunlap, 1980), 48.

15. B. Fisher, *Rebuilding*, 6.

16. Richard P. Olson and Carole Della Pia-Terry, *Ministry with Remarried Persons* (Valley Forge, Penn.: Judson Press, 1984), 46.

17. Ibid.,

18. William D. Horton, "The Re-marriage of Divorcees in Church," *Expository Times* 93 (January 1982): 108.

19. Judith Tate O'Brien and Gene O'Brien, *A Redeeming State: A Handbook for Couples Planning Remarriage in the Church* (Ramsey, N.J.: Paulist Press, 1983).

20. Olson and Pia-Terry, *Ministry*, 129–46. See also their workbook for remarried couples, *Help for Remarried Couples and Families* (Valley Forge, Penn.: Judson Press, 1984).

21. August B. Hollingshead, "Marital Status and Wedding Behavior," *Marriage and Family Living* (November 1952): 311.

22. See Knight, *Second Marriage*; Susan H. Fields, *Getting Married Again* (New York: Dodd, Mead, and Co., 1975); and Marjabelle Young Stewart, *New Etiquette Guide to Getting Married Again* (New York: Avon Books, 1981).

23. Selina Sue Prosen and Jay H. Farmer, "Understanding Stepfamilies: Issues and Implications for Counselors," *The Personnel and Guidance Journal* 60 (March 1982): 393.

24. Capon, *A Second Day*, 111.

25. Olson and Pia-Terry, *Ministry*, 64–65.

26. Robert Perske ["That Second Marriage Service: A Pastoral Worksheet," *The Journal of Pastoral Care* 28 (March 1974): 17–22] has some excellent suggestions for couples wishing to write their own re-marriage rituals.

27. Hesse, "Stages."

28. Elie Wiesel, *Messengers of God: Biblical Portraits and Legends* (New York: Random House, 1976), 32.
29. Leslie Aldridge Westoff, *The Second Time Around: Remarriage in America* (New York: Penguin Books, 1978), 169.
30. Myron Madden, *The Power to Bless* (Nashville: Broadman Press, 1970), 15.

VII. What Can Be Expected of Clergy When Divorce Occurs

1. Earl A. Grollman, "Clergy of Limited Use in Divorce Counseling, Rabbi Declares," *Marriage and Divorce Today* 3 (March 27, 1978): 2
2. Richard A. Kulka, Joseph Veroff, and Elizabeth Douvan, "Social Class and the Use of Professional Help for Personal Problems," *Journal of Health and Social Behavior* 20 (March 1979): 2–17.
3. Daniel Day Williams, *The Minister and the Care of Souls* (New York: Harper and Row, 1961), 147.
4. William A. Clebsch and Charles R. Jaekle, *Pastoral Care in Historical Perspective* (Englewood Cliffs, N.J.: Prentice-Hall, 1964), 4.
5. Weiss, *Marital Separation*, 14f.
6. Emily M. Brown, "Divorce Counseling" in *Treating Relationships*, ed. David H. L. Olson, (Lake Mills, Iowa: Graphic Publishing Company, 1976), 399. Divorce therapy is discussed in Kenneth Kressel and Morton Deutsch, "Divorce Therapy: An In-depth Survey of Therapists' Views," *Family Process* 16 (December 1977): 413–43.
7. The following referral resources can provide names of qualified therapists:

   American Association for Marriage and Family Therapy
   1717 K Street NW #407
   Washington, D.C. 20006
   Tel. (202) 429–1825

   Family Service Association of America
   44 East 23rd Street
   New York, New York 10010
   Tel. (212) 674–6100

   American Association of Pastoral Counselors
   9508 Lee Highway
   Fairfax, Virginia 22031
   Tel. (703) 385–7967

   Family Mediation Association
   5018 Allan Road
   Washington, D.C. 20016
8. Kessler, *Beyond Divorce: Leader's Guide*, (Atlanta, Ga.: National Institute of Professional Training, 1977), 17–18.

9. E. Fisher, "A Guide to Divorce Counseling," *The Family Coordinator* 22 (January 1973): 55–61.

10. Richard L. Krebs, "Why Pastors Should Not Be Counselors," *The Journal of Pastoral Care* 34 (December 1980): 229–33.

11. Ibid., 229–30.

12. David K. Switzer, "Why Pastors *Should* Be Counselors (Of a Sort): A Response to Richard L. Krebs," *The Journal of Pastoral Care* 37 (March 1983): 28–32.

13. Ibid., 29.

14. Reprinted with permission from Weiss, R. L. & Cerreto, M. C. "The Marital Status Inventory: Development of a Measure of Dissolution Potential," *The American Journal of Family Therapy,* 1980, 8(2), 80–85, © Brunner/Mazel, Inc. When interpreting the MSI, the following guidelines are suggested: persons who mark Items 1 and 2 as True have only occasional thoughts about divorce. Persons who mark Items 3 and 12 as True and 5 and 10 as False have serious intentions of separation. Persons who mark 11 and 13 as False are seeking legal advice while those marking Items 8 and 14 as True have filed for separation or divorce.

15. Marjorie Kawin Toomin, "Structured Separation with Counseling: A Therapeutic Approach for Couples in Conflict," *Family Process* 2 (September 1972): 299–310.

16. J. C. Wynn, *Family Therapy in Pastoral Ministry* (San Francisco: Harper and Row, 1982), 109.

17. Norman Sheresky and Marya Mannes, *Uncoupling: The Art of Coming Apart* (New York: Viking Press, 1972), xi.

18. O. J. Coogler, *Structured Mediation in Divorce Settlement* (Lexington, Mass.: Lexington Books, 1978).

19. Robert B. Coates, "A Ministry of Mediation: The Divorce Settlement," *The Journal of Pastoral Care* 37 (December 1983): 272.

20. Roger Fisher and William Ury, *Getting to YES: Negotiating Agreement Without Giving In* (New York: Penguin Books, 1983), 14.

21. Janet Weinglass, Kenneth Kressel, and Morton Deutsch, "The Role of the Clergy in Divorce: An Exploratory Survey," *Journal of Divorce* 2 (Fall 1978): 76.

22. Donald Capps, *Pastoral Counseling and Preaching: A Quest for an Integrated Ministry* (Philadelphia: The Westminster Press, 1980).

23. William H. Willimon, *Integrative Preaching: The Pulpit at the Center* (Nashville: Abingdon Press, 1981), 49. See also William V. Arnold, "Preach on Marriage and Divorce, Pastor," in *Journal for Preachers,* VII (Lent 1984): 2–6 for some excellent suggestions for preaching about divorce in the context of marriage.

24. David Dalke, *The Healing Divorce: A Practical and Theological Approach* (Tapes covering 10 sessions and workbook, *Healing Divorce Guide-*

book, available from Learnings Unlimited, 516 4th Avenue, Longmont, Colo. 80501).

25. Nouwen, *The Wounded Healer*, 42. Copyright © 1972 by Henri J. M. Nouwen. Reprinted by permission of Doubleday and Company, Inc.

26. Ibid., 89.

27. David R. Mace, "The Pastor and Divorce," *Pastoral Psychology* 9 (September 1958): 65. Copyright © 1958 by Human Sciences Press, 72 Fifth Avenue, New York, N.Y. 10011. Reprinted by permission.

VIII. The Church Reconstructs Broken Lives

1. G. Edwin Bontrager, *Divorce and the Faithful Church* (Scottsdale, Pa.: Herald Press, 1978), 81.

2. Karl Heim, *Christian Faith and Natural Science*, trans. N. Horton Smith (New York: Harper and Brothers), 1953, 28.

3. Vande Kemp and Schreck, "The Church's Ministry to Singles," 151. Reprinted by permission of Human Sciences Press, Inc.

4. Ibid., 153.

5. Jürgen Moltmann, *The Power of the Powerless* (San Francisco: Harper and Row, 1983), 104.

6. Edwin Markham, *Outwitted*. Reprinted with permission of Virgil Markham.

7. Rambo, *The Divorcing Christian*, 48.

8. Kysar, *The Asundered*, 105–106.

9. Walter Wangerin, "On Mourning the Death of a Marriage," *Christianity Today* 28 (May 18, 1984): 22, 23.

10. Westerhoff and Willimon, *Liturgy and Learning*, 129.

11. Don S. Browning, *The Moral Context of Pastoral Care* (Philadelphia: The Westminster Press, 1976), 109.

12. William B. Oglesby, Jr., *Biblical Themes for Pastoral Care* (Nashville: Abingdon Press, 1980), 39–40.

13. Diane Detwiler-Zapp and William Caveness Dixon, *Lay Caregiving* (Philadelphia: Fortress Press, 1982).

14. Howard W. Stone, *The Caring Church: A Guide for Lay Pastoral Care* (San Francisco: Harper and Row, 1983).

15. Rambo, "Ministry with the Divorcing," *Pacific Theological Review* 17 (Winter 1984): 17.

16. Nouwen, *The Wounded Healer*, 95. Reprinted by permission of Doubleday and Company, Inc.

17. Thomas R. Kelly, *A Testament of Devotion* (New York: Harper and Brothers, 1941), 85–86.

18. Vande Kemp and Schreck, "The Church's Ministry to Singles," 153.

19. John Slyker, "Life in These United States," *Reader's Digest* (March 1984), 69. Copyright © Reader's Digest. Reprinted with permission from the March 1984 Reader's Digest.

20. Monica J. Maxon, "Caring as a Calling," *The Christian Century* 101 (January 25, 1984): 93.
21. Ibid.
22. Quoted in Roland H. Bainton, *What Christianity Says About Sex, Love, and Marriage* (New York: Association Press, 1951), 102.
23. Ibid., 101.

For Further Reading

Titles used in this book, as well as a few others especially apt for this book's intended readers, are included.

The Divorce Process

Arnold, William V. *Divorce: Prevention or Survival*. Philadelphia: The Westminster Press, 1981.

Bohannan, Paul, ed. *Divorce and After*. Garden City, N.Y.: Doubleday and Company, 1971.

Correu, Larry M., *Beyond the Broken Marriage*. Philadelphia: The Westminster Press, 1982.

Kessler, Sheila. *The American Way of Divorce: Prescriptions for Change* Chicago: Nelson-Hall, 1975.

Krantzler, Mel. *Creative Divorce*. New York: New American Library, 1975.

Ripple, Paula. *The Pain and the Possibility: Divorce and Separation Among Catholics*. Notre Dame: Ave Maria Press, 1978.

Trafford, Abigail. *Crazy Time: Surviving Divorce*. New York: Harper and Row, 1982.

Weiss, Robert S. *Marital Separation*. New York: Basic Books, 1975.

A Christian Theology of Divorce

Atkinson, David. *To Have and To Hold: The Marriage Covenant and the Discipline of Divorce*. Grand Rapids, Mich.: William B. Eerdmans Press, 1979.

Bontrager, G. Edwin. *Divorce and the Faithful Church*. Scottsdale, Pa.: Herald Press, 1978.

Ellisen, Stanley A. *Divorce and Remarriage in the Church*. Grand Rapids, Mich.: Zondervan, 1980.

Kelleher, Stephen J. *Divorce and Remarriage for Catholics?* New York: Doubleday, 1973.

Kelly, Kevin T. *Divorce and Second Marriage: Facing the Challenge*. New York: The Seabury Press, 1983.

Kysar, Myrna and Robert. *The Asundered: Biblical Teachings on Divorce and Remarriage*. Atlanta: John Knox Press, 1978.

Rambo, Lewis R. *The Divorcing Christian*. Nashville: Abingdon Press, 1983.

Shaner, Donald W. *A Christian View of Divorce According to the Teachings of the New Testament*. Leiden, Netherlands: E. J. Brill, 1969.

Woodson, Les. *Divorce and the Gospel of Grace*. Waco, Tex.: Word Books, 1979.

The Church's Ministry to the Divorced

Brown, Raymond Kay. *Reach out to Singles: A Challenge to Ministry*. Philadelphia: The Westminster Press, 1979.

Christoff, Nicholas, B. *Saturday Night, Sunday Morning: Singles and the Church*. New York: Harper and Row, 1978.

Emerson, James G., Jr. *Divorce, The Church, and Remarriage*. Philadelphia: The Westminster Press, 1961.

Landgraf, John R. *Creative Singlehood and Pastoral Care*. Philadelphia: Fortress Press, 1982.

Lyon, William. *A Pew for One, Please: The Church and the Single Person*. New York: The Seabury Press, 1977.

Young, James J. *Divorcing, Believing, Belonging*. Ramsey, N.J.: Paulist Press, 1984.

Divorce Counseling and Divorce Groups

Bernard, Janine M. and Harold Hackney. *Untying the Knot: A Guide to Civilized Divorce*. Minneapolis, Minn: Winston Press, 1983.

Brown, Emily. "Divorce Counseling." In *Treating Relationships*, ed. David H. L. Olson. Lake Mills, Iowa: Graphic Publishing Co., 1976.

Fisher, Bruce. *Rebuilding: When Your Relationship Ends*. San Luis Obispo, Calif.: Impact Publishers, 1981.

Fisher, Esther Oshiver. *Divorce: The New Freedom*. New York: Harper and Row, 1974.

Schneider, Karen L. and Myles J. *Divorce Mediation: The Constructive New Way to End a Marriage*. Washington, D.C.: Acropolis Press, 1984.

Spaniol, LeRoy J., and Paul A. Lannan. *Getting Unstuck: Moving On After Divorce*. Ramsey, N.J.: Paulist Press, 1984.

The Church's Ministry to the Remarried

Capon, Robert Farrar. *A Second Day: Reflections on Remarriage*. New York: William Morrow and Company, 1980.

Cauhapé, Elizabeth. *Fresh Starts: Men and Women After Divorce*. New York: Basic Books, 1983.

Mackin, Theodore. *Divorce and Remarriage*. Ramsey, N.J.: Paulist Press, 1984.

Mynatt, Elaine S. *Remarriage Reality: What You Can Learn From It*. Knoxville, Tenn.: Elms Publishing Co., 1984.

O'Brien, Judith Tate, and Gene O'Brien. *A Redeeming State: A Handbook for Couples Planning Remarriage in the Church*. Ramsey, N.J.: Paulist Press, 1983.

Olson, Richard P., and Carole Della Pia-Terry. *Ministry with Remarried Persons*. Valley Forge, Pa.: Judson Press, 1984.

—————. *Help for Remarried Couples and Families*. Valley Forge, Pa.: Judson Press, 1984.

Sills, Judith. *How to Stop Looking for Someone Perfect and Find Someone to Love*. New York: St. Martins Press, 1984.

Small, Dwight Hervey. *The Right to Remarry*. Old Tappan, N.J.: Fleming H. Revell, 1977.

Westoff, Leslie Aldridge. *The Second Time Around: Remarriage in America*. New York: Penguin Books, 1978.

The Church Restructures Broken Lives

Brister, C. W. *Pastoral Care in the Church*. New York: Harper and Row, 1964.

Bryant, Marcus D. *The Art of Christian Caring*. St. Louis, Mo.: The Bethany Press, 1979.

Detwiler-Zapp, Diane, and William Caveness Dixon. *Lay Caregiving*. Philadelphia: Fortress Press, 1982.

Oglesby, William B., Jr. *Biblical Themes for Pastoral Care*. Nashville: Abingdon Press, 1980.

Stone, Howard W. *The Caring Church: A Guide for Lay Pastoral Care*. San Francisco: Harper and Row, 1983.

Westerhoff, John H. III. *Inner Growth, Outer Change*. New York: The Seabury Press, 1979.

Westerhoff, John H. III, and William H. Willimon. *Liturgy and Learning Through the Life Cycle*. New York: The Seabury Press, 1980.

Index of Names and Subjects

Index of Biblical References